TEACHINGS OF THE

JEWISH MYSTICS

Compiled and edited by

PERLE BESSERMAN

SHAMBHALA

Boston & London

1998

SHAMBHALA PUBLICATIONS, INC.
Horticultural Hall
300 Massachusetts Avenue
Boston, Massachusetts 02115
www.shambhala.com

9   8   7   6   5   4   3   2   1

PRINTED IN UNITED STATES
⊗ This edition is printed on acid-free paper that meets
the American National Standards Institute z39.48 Standard.
Distributed in the United States by Random House, Inc.,
and in Canada by Random House of Canada Ltd

Library of Congress Cataloging-in-Publication Data
Way of the Jewish mystics.
Teachings of the Jewish mystics/edited by Perle Besserman.
p.   cm.
Previously published: The way of the Jewish mystics. Boston:
Shambhala: [New York]: Distributed in the United States by
Random House, 1994.
Includes bibliographical references.
ISBN 1-57062-351-1 (paperback: alk. paper)
1. Mysticism—Judaism—Quotations, maxims,
etc.   I. Besserman, Perle.   II. Title.
BM723.W34   1994   97-42458
296.7′12—dc21   CIP

In memory of

ARYEH KAPLAN

Contents

INTRODUCTION

JEWISH MYSTICS tread the earth lightly. Steeped in the immediacy of the moment, witness to the blessings of birdsong and bread, they embody their wisdom and teach by the way they live. Very often they are wanderers, traveling from town to town along the dusty roads from Safed to Jerusalem or the winding valleys of the Carpathian Mountains, talking, selling shoelaces and buttons as they go. Some are legendary, empowered by heaven to gather entire assemblies aboard an angel's wing and lecture before the fiery throne of the boundless One. Others, borne aloft by a simple melody, shower love across the face of a hard and loveless world. All are egoless, light; they sparkle and dance, tell stories with words that shimmer and weep.

Their creed is as old as Eden. Their prayers and contemplations are the stuff of creation. Fearless, hungry for knowledge, they climb the Tree of Life and gaze where lesser folk dare not. They cavort with Abraham and the Heavenly Host, with misers and kings; all interest them equally. They are citizens of a borderless country on pilgrimage through the myriad worlds. Their mother is Torah, their map the commandments. The dazzling spheres of light on the cosmic tree guide them along the way. "Come see!" the mystics call to the busy passerby and the dreamer alike, liberating those who would follow from the narrow cage of self.

Gathering in quorums of firs and beeches, they pray, fall in love, scream in silence, bless the grass, turn childlike. Calling themselves "Cubs" and their leader "Lion," they rise at midnight to hunt for spiritual food. As dervishes and scribes, they haunt the cobbled streets of Spain with the spinning hum of the Holy Name. Donning sackcloth and smearing their faces with ash, they mourn the shattered vessels of divine constriction, hoping to patch them with their tears. They talk in riddles, tongues, and parables. Holy nonsense. They dance, court the Sabbath Queen, laugh at themselves; they are sometimes born with the healing touch. Often they die young, in faraway places, before their time.

Two, a father and son, are fugitives; they sit buried to the neck in sand, foreheads scorched by the Near Eastern sun. A miracle: a spring and carob tree appear, offering shade and refreshment. An angel disguised as a donkey driver passes by and engages them in divine discourse.

A wandering Polish preacher seeks out the Master of the Holy Name and finds a country oaf. As the preacher turns to leave, the bumpkin speaks. The room fills with blinding light, the scholarly preacher is overcome, and a lineage is born.

A loyal scribe writes on a palm leaf, scribbles by sputtering candlelight in a secret diary, cups his ear for the whisper of his teacher's spirit-guide from across the Sabbath table, passes down words, formulas, letters, unifications, warnings to solitary travelers in the mystic realm. The tradition is conveyed "from mouth to ear." There is no tradition. There are no textbooks. There is only direct meeting, direct experience. There is no practice without a teacher. There is no teacher without a community. There are souls destined to meet—and free will and commitment, and loving-kindness and fellowship. And out of these branches the path.

EDITOR'S NOTE

WITH FEW exceptions, the spellings of Hebrew words, names, and titles appear as they do in the original texts from which this anthology has been drawn and therefore vary in many instances. Another occasional inconsistency is in the citations from the Hebrew Bible, which has been codified in a variety of ways, so that they may not always correspond to the numbering in other translations of the Bible.

Teachings of the
Jewish Mystics

NATURE

How wonderful it would be if one could only be worthy of hearing the song of the grass. Each blade of grass sings out to God without any ulterior motive and without expecting any reward. It is most wonderful to hear its song and worship God in its midst.

The best place to meditate is in a field where things grow. There one can truly express his thoughts before God. . . .

The best place to meditate is in the meadows outside the city. One should meditate in a grassy field, for grass will awaken the heart.

NACHMAN OF BRATZLAV (*trans. Aryeh Kaplan*)

◈

Once when Rabbi Kook was walking in the fields, lost deep in thought, the young student with him inadvertently plucked a leaf off a branch. Rabbi Kook was visibly shaken by this act, and turning to his companion he said gently: "Believe me when I tell you that I never simply pluck a leaf or a blade of grass or any living thing unless I have to. Every part of the vegetable world is singing a song and breathing forth a secret of the divine mystery of the creation." The

I

words of Rabbi Kook penetrated deeply into the mind of the young student. For the first time he understood what it means to show compassion to all creatures.

ALAN UNTERMAN

◈

MY MASTER of blessed memory [Isaac Luria] used to be careful never to destroy any insect, even the smallest and least significant among them, such as fleas and gnats, bees and the like, even if they were annoying him.

HAYIM VITAL (*trans. Lawrence Fine*)

◈

TAKE ONLY enough food and drink as you require for your sustenance, and abstain from anything beyond this. The subtle tactic to adopt in this regard is to diminish the number of different prepared courses and limit yourself to one course only, if you are able to do so. Accustom yourself to do occasionally without such food so as to control your appetite, and learn to be contented when it is withheld from you. If, however, you are able to forgo such prepared food entirely, which entails labor and effort in its preparation, and can rely upon that food which requires no exertion whatsoever, such as olives and grapes and the like, do so. . . .

Regard what you eat as being for your health rather than as a food. Your drink should consist of water only, unless your purpose in taking wine is to improve your physical health or to dispel anxiety from your heart. Be careful not to drink wine often, or to excess, and desist from taking up with drinking parties, since such behavior is a great detriment to the practice of Torah and religious devotion.

BAHYA IBN PAQUDA (*trans. Lawrence Fine*)

❖

THERE IS nothing so beloved by the Holy One, blessed be He, as the Incense. It is able to banish sorcery and all evil influences from the house. Seeing that perfumes prepared by men possess the virtue to counteract, by their odor and fumes, the ill effects of evil things, how much more so the Incense! It is a firmly established ordinance of the Holy One, blessed be He, that whoever reflects on and recites daily the section of the Incense will be saved from all evil things.

ZOHAR (*trans. Lawrence Fine*)

❖

WHEN NOAH came out of the ark
he opened his eyes and saw the whole world completely
    destroyed.
He began crying for the world and said,
"Master of the world!
If You destroyed Your world because of human sin or
    human fools,
then why did You create them?
One or the other You should do:

either do not create the human being
or do not destroy the world!"
He offered up offerings and began to pray before Him
and the aroma ascended before the Blessed Holy One and
    was sweet. . . .
A triple aroma ascended to God:
the aroma of Noah's offering, the aroma of his prayer,
and the aroma of his actions.
No aroma in the whole world was as pleasing to Him.
Therefore He commanded:
"Be observant and present to Me in due season My pleasing
    aroma" (Numbers 28:2).
This means:
"Be observant:
Present to Me the aroma that Noah presented to Me:
the aroma of offering and prayer and right action."

                ZOHAR (*trans. Daniel Chanan Matt*)

❖

ON HIS second journey to [Mezeritch], young [Shneur] Zalman [of Liadi] visited Rabbi Pinhas of Koretz. Rabbi Pinhas wanted to teach him the language of birds and the language of plants, but the younger man refused. "There is only *one* thing men need understand," he said.

In his old age, Rabbi Shneur Zalman was once driving through the country with his grandson. Birds were hopping about and twittering everywhere. The rabbi put his head out of the carriage for a while. "How fast they chatter," he said to the child. "They have their own alphabet. All you need to do is listen and grasp well, and you will understand their language."

MARTIN BUBER

❖

THE MAIN reason that God sends the soul to this lowly physical body is because He has very great pleasure and delight from this.

The soul is in a very filthy vessel, since [man was created out of the "dust of the earth"] and there is nothing lower and less spiritual than dust. Still, [this lowly physical body] constantly gives praise and thanks to its Creator. This is very remarkable.

God has more delight from this praise than from all the worship and songs of the angels. The angels do not have gross bodies, and for them [such worship] is not at all remarkable.

THE BAAL SHEM TOV (trans. Aryeh Kaplan)

❖

THE HOLY Rabbi Dov Baer [the Maggid of Mezeritch] asked, "How was the Garden of Eden created before man? Is it not true that each person creates his own Garden of Eden through his good deeds? This being so, where was this Garden of Eden before man was created?"

He explained that for God, past and future are exactly the same—"He looks and sees until the end of all generations."

The delight that God has from the righteous who would do His will therefore existed even before the righteous were created. This delight came before God, causing Him to create the Garden of Eden.

AVRAHAM CHAIM OF ZLATCHOV (*trans. Aryeh Kaplan*)

❖

PEOPLE DO not consider the ability to forget an advantage. But without it, it would be impossible to live in this world.

Imagine that you would constantly recall all that we know about the future world.

There is an angel with a thousand heads.

Each head has a thousand tongues.

Each tongue has a thousand voices.

Each voice has a thousand melodies.

Imagine the indescribable beauty of this angel's song. If you could imagine such things without forgetting, you would constantly be comparing your own limited abilities to the immensity of such a being. It would be utterly impossible for you to endure life. You would be so disgusted with your worldly life that you would die before your time.

NACHMAN OF BRATZLAV (*trans. Aryeh Kaplan*)

PRAYER

THE FIRST requisite is setting the atmosphere. The many
laws regarding the respect that one must have for the synagogue are designed to make the synagogue a place with a
worshipful, meditative atmosphere. Just walking into the
synagogue should be an experience that prepares a person
to commune with his Maker. Merely being there should be
enough to remove all extraneous thoughts from one's mind.

. . . One would do well to emulate the many Sephardim
who do not utter a single irrelevant word from the time they
enter the synagogue until they leave. [Keeping] synagogue
conversation to a minimum is absolutely essential if one
expects to learn how to develop *kavanah*. . . . The word has
variously been translated as "feeling," "emotion," "concentration," or "devotion." Its root, however, is *kiven*, which
means "to aim," suggesting "directed consciousness" as per-
haps the most literal translation of *kavanah*. Indeed, it does
consist of directing all of one's thoughts toward a single
goal.

ARYEH KAPLAN

❖

7

[RABBI NACHMAN prayed in] Yiddish. He would find a secluded place and set it aside to express his thoughts to [God].

Speaking in his own language, he would beg and plead before [God]. He would make use of all sorts of arguments and logic, crying that it was fitting that [God] draw him close and help him in his devotion. He kept this up constantly, spending days and years engaged in such prayer.

His father's house had a small garret, partitioned off as a storehouse for hay and feed. Here young Rabbi Nachman would hide himself, chanting the Psalms and screaming quietly, begging [God] that he be worthy of drawing himself close to Him.

Besides this, the Rebbe made use of every published prayer he could find. He went through all the books of prayers available, and there was not a prayer that he did not repeat countless times. . . . He poured out his heart in every possible prayer and supplication, even those printed in Yiddish for women. . . . He would say the prayers for all seven days of the week at one time. . . .

But beyond all this, the main thing was his own prayers, emanating from his heart in his own language. He would pray and argue before [God], making up petitions and arguments as he went along. He would beg and plead that [God] make him worthy of true devotion.

ARYEH KAPLAN

❖

EACH LETTER is ruled by an angel [representing] a ray of an outflow of the virtues of the Almightiness and qualities of God. The angels which dwell in the earthly and in the heavenly world rule those who abide in our earthly one. The letters form the words, then the words the prayers, and it is the angels who, designated by the letters and assembled in the written and spoken words, work the wonders at which ordinary men are amazed.

SIEGMUND HURWITZ

❖

"HEAR O Israel, the Lord is our God, the Lord is One"—proclaims His unity from the heights to the depths, and from the depths to the heights. . . . You should be aware that our Rabbis, may their memories be blessed, established that one should say "Blessed be the name of the Glory of His Kingdom . . . forever and always" in the recitation of the Shema. They established that it should be said because Jacob said it, but it should be said in a whisper because Moses, peace be upon him, did not say it.

They told a parable: To what is this compared? To the king's daughter who smelled minced meat pudding [and desired it]. If [her servant] mentions the odor, she will be embarrassed. If she says nothing, she will suffer. [So] her servants began to secretly bring her some of it.

JACOB BEN SHESHET OF GERONA
(*trans. Ronald C. Kiener*)

❖

ONCE TOWARDS the close of the Day of Atonement, when Jews fast and pray for twenty-five hours, Rabbi Levi Isaac of Berditchev felt that through his prayers he had almost succeeded in bringing about the Messiah. So he began to put a last great effort into his prayers in order to complete the task. Suddenly he became aware that there was a Jew in the synagogue, very faint from fasting, and that if he, Rabbi Levi Isaac, delayed the conclusion of the prayers any longer the man would die. So Rabbi Levi Isaac quickly concluded the synagogue service and declared the fast at an end. The effort to bring about the coming of the Messiah had to be abandoned.

ALAN UNTERMAN

❖

WHEN A person is drowning and thrashes about to save himself, people certainly will not make fun of his motions.

Similarly, when a person makes motions during prayer, one should not laugh at him. He is saving himself from drowning in the Waters of Insolence . . . coming to prevent him from concentrating on his prayers.

THE BAAL SHEM TOV (trans. Aryeh Kaplan)

❖

DURING THE first part of the night [when the Safed mystics pray and] the rite for Rachel takes place, an individual laments the exile of the Shekhinah [female aspect of God] by engaging in acts of mourning: removal of shoes, weeping, placing ashes on one's forehead, and rubbing one's eyes in the dust on the ground in order to symbolize the Shekhinah, who lies in the dust Herself. The adept then recites Psalm 137, which recalls the Babylonian exile, Psalm 79, the final chapter of the Book of Lamentations, and other songs of lament. This is followed by the rite for Leah, in which attention shifts to the theme of redemption. During this part of the ritual hymns that look forward to the coming of the Messiah are sung. Finally, the rite for the soul is celebrated, in which one contemplatively seeks to restore the unity of Tiferet [Beauty] [with] Shekhinah.

LAWRENCE FINE

❖

THERE WILL be many times that one will find it impossible to say anything to God. His mouth will be sealed, and he will not be able to find any words to say. Nevertheless, the very fact that he has made the effort and has prepared himself to converse with God is in itself very beneficial. He has tried, and is ready and prepared to converse with God, yearning and longing to do so, but he is unable. This in itself is also very good.

Actually, one can make a conversation and prayer out of this itself. He should cry out to God that he is so far from Him that he cannot even speak. He should beg that God grant him mercy and open his mouth, so that he will be able to express himself before Him.

NACHMAN OF BRATZLAV (trans. Aryeh Kaplan)

❖

WHERE I wander—You!
Where I ponder—You!
Only You everywhere, You, always You.
You, You, You.
When I am gladdened—You!
And when I am saddened—You!
Only You, everywhere You!
You, You, You.
Sky is You!
Earth is You!
You above! You below!
In every trend, at every end,
Only You, everywhere You!
LEVI YITZCHAK OF BERDITCHOV (*trans. Harry Rabinowicz*)

◈

THERE WAS once an illiterate cowherd who did not know
how to pray, so instead he would say to God: "Master of
the Universe, you know that if you had cows and you gave
them to me to look after I would do it for nothing, even
though I take wages from everyone else. I would do it for
you for nothing because I love you." A certain sage chanced
upon the cowherd and heard him praying in this manner.
The sage said to him, "You fool, you must not pray like
that." The cowherd asked him how he should pray, and the
sage set about teaching him the order of prayers as they
are found in the prayerbook. After the sage went away the

cowherd soon forgot what he had been taught and so he did not pray at all. He was afraid to say his usual prayer about God's cows because the sage had told him that it was wrong to say such things, on the other hand he could not say what the sage had told him because it was all jumbled up in his mind. That night the sage was reprimanded in a dream and told that unless the cowherd returned to his spontaneous prayer great harm would befall the sage, for he had stolen something very precious away from God. On awakening the sage hurried back to the cowherd and asked him what he was praying. The cowherd told him that he was not praying anything since he had forgotten the prayers the sage had taught him, and he had been forbidden to tell God how he would look after his cows for nothing. The sage begged him to forget what he had told him and to go back to his real prayers that he had said before ever he had met him.

JUDAH THE PIETIST (*trans. Alan Unterman*)

Vision and Prophecy

CONCENTRATE ON the image of the letter *alef* [א] with your eyes and understand it in your heart. You will find that many hidden truths concerning the shapes of other letters are depicted and encompassed in the shape of the *alef*— something you will not find in any other letter.

. . . The *alef* is the first letter pronounced in the mouth with air, without any strain or effort, to teach that the Holy One, blessed be He, is one with no other partner, that He is hidden from all creatures. Just as the *alef* is pronounced in a hidden and concealed spot at the back of the tongue, so the Holy One, blessed be He, is hidden from visible sight. Similarly, just as the *alef* is ethereal and imperceptible, so the Holy One, blessed be He, denied to all creatures the ability to comprehend Him, save by means of thought, for thought is pure and unblemished and subtle as the ether. . . .

Thus we learn from the image of the *alef,* within which the shapes of all letters are hidden, that there is no creature without a Creator, no handiwork without a Maker, and no depiction without an Illustrator.

JACOB BEN JACOB HA-KOHEN (*trans. Ronald C. Kiener*)

◈

WHENEVER YOU wish that [Elijah] become visible to you, concentrate [on him] at bedtime. There are three ways of seeing him: in a dream, . . . while awake and greeting him, . . . while awake, greeting him, and being greeted in return.

JOSEPH CARO (*trans. Aryeh Kaplan*)

◇

COME AND see:
Certain colors can be seen;
certain colors cannot.
These and those are the high mystery of faith.
But human beings do not know; they do not reflect.

The colors that can be seen—
no one was pure enough to see them
until the Patriarchs came and mastered them.
Therefore the word *appeared,*
for they saw the colors which are revealed.
Which are revealed?
Colors of El Shaddai, colors in a cosmic prism.
These can be seen.

But the colors above,
hidden and invisible—
no human has mastered them except for Moses.
Therefore the verse concludes:
"But by My name YHVH, I was not known to them."
I was not revealed to them in high colors. . . .

Come and see:
There are four lights.
Three are concealed and one is revealed.
A shining light.
A glowing light;
it shines like the clear brilliance of heaven.
A purple light that absorbs all lights.
A light that does not shine
but gazes toward the others and draws them in. . . .

The secret is: the eye.
Come and see:
Three colors appear in the eye,
but none of them glow,
for they are overshadowed by a light that does not shine.
These are images of the colors that are hidden, which
oversee them. . . .

The secret is: close your eye and roll your eyeball.
Those colors that shine and glow will be revealed.
Permission to see is granted only with eyes concealed,
for they are high and concealed,
overseeing those colors that can be seen but do not glow.

ZOHAR (*trans. Daniel Chanan Matt*)

❖

"PREPARE TO meet your God, O Israel." Prepare yourself,
unify your heart, and purify your body. Choose a special
place for yourself, where your voice will not be heard by

anyone else. Meditate . . . alone, with no one else present. Sit in one place in a room or attic. Do not reveal your secret to anyone.

If you engage in this by day, do so in a darkened room. It is best, however, that you do it at night.

At this time, when you prepare yourself to speak to your Creator and you desire to witness His might, be careful to cleanse your thoughts of all worldly folly.

Wrap yourself in your Tallit [prayer shawl]. If the time is proper, also place your Tefillin [phylacteries] on your head and arm. This will increase your awe and trembling before the Divine Presence which will visit you at this time.

Wear clean clothing. If possible, all your clothing should be white. This is of great help for one's concentration on fear and love [of God].

If it is at night, light many candles, so that your eyes are well illuminated.

Then take in your hand a tablet and some ink. These will serve as your witnesses that you are coming to serve God with joy and good heart.

Then begin to permute a number of letters. You may use only a few, or you may use many. Transpose and permute them quickly, until your heart is warmed as a result of these permutations, their motions, and what is derived from these permutations.

As a result of these permutations, your heart will become extremely warm. From the permutations, you will gain new knowledge that you never learned from human traditions nor derived from intellectual analysis. When you experience this, you are prepared to receive the influx. . . .

The influx will then come, bestowed to you. It will arouse in you many words, one after the other.

Then prepare your inner thoughts to depict God and His highest angels. Depict them in your heart as if they were human beings sitting or standing around you. You are in their midst, like a messenger whom the King and His servants wish to send on a mission. You are ready to hear the words of the message, whether it is from the King or from one of His servants, from His mouth, or from the mouth of any one of them. . . .

The divine influx will begin to prevail in you, and will weaken your external and internal organs. Your entire body will begin to tremble, until you think that you are about to die. This is because your soul is separating itself from your body as a result of the great joy that you experience when you perceive and recognize these things. . . .

At that time, you may wish to honor the glorious Name and serve Him with the life of your body and soul. Conceal your face, and be afraid to gaze upon God. "Do not come closer. Remove your shoes from your feet, for the place upon which you stand is holy ground" (Exodus 3:5).

Instead, involve yourself with your body once again. Stand up, eat something, drink something, smell a pleasant fragrance, and let your spirit once again return to its sheath.

ABRAHAM ABULAFIA (*trans. Aryeh Kaplan*)

❖

THERE WAS a king who created, through his magical art, barriers and walls, one within the other, with which to surround himself. All these were, however, really illusory. He commanded that money be spread around at the gates of each of these walls to see how great the determination and desire of his subjects, how much effort each one of them would make, to come to the king. There were those of his subjects who immediately returned home after they had collected a little money at the gates of these illusory walls. There were others who got as far as the second or third walls. But there were very few who did not desire to collect merely physical treasures, only to reach the king himself. After considerable effort they came to the king and saw that there were really no barriers and walls, everything was a magical illusion. So it is with God. Those who truly understand know that all the barriers and walls of iron, all the garments and coverings are really only God himself in hiding, as it were, because there is no place where he is not.

THE BAAL SHEM TOV (*trans. Alan Unterman*)

❖

THE SPARK expanded, whirling round and round.
Sparks burst into flashes and rose high above.
The heavens blazed with all their powers;
everything flashed and sparkled as one.
Then the spark turned from the side of the South
and outlined a curve from there to the East
and from the East to the North
until it had circled back to the South, as before.
Then the spark swirled, disappearing;
comets and flashes dimmed.

Now they came forth, these carved, flaming letters
flashing like gold when it dazzles.
Like a craftsman smelting silver and gold:
when he takes them out of the blazing fire
all is bright and pure;
so the letters came forth, pure and bright
from the flowing measure of the spark.
Therefore it is written:
"The word of YHVH is refined" (Psalm 18:31),
as silver and gold are refined.
When these letters came forth, they were all refined,
carved precisely, sparkling, flashing.
All of Israel saw the letters
flying through space in every direction,
engraving themselves on the tablets of stone.

ZOHAR (*trans. Daniel Chanan Matt*)

◆

It is told:

In Lublin the Afternoon Prayer was delayed even on the Sabbath. Before this prayer, the rabbi sat alone in his room every Sabbath, and no one was permitted to enter it. Once a Hasid hid there to find out what happened on these occasions. All he saw at first was that the rabbi seated himself at the table and opened a book. But then a vast light began to shine in the narrow room, and when he saw it the Hasid became unconscious. He came to himself when the rabbi left the room, and he too went out as soon as he fully regained consciousness. In the entrance, he saw nothing, but he heard them saying the evening prayer and realized with horror that the candles must be lit and that he, notwithstanding, was surrounded by utter darkness. He was terrified, implored the rabbi to help him, and was sent to another city, to a man who was known to perform miraculous cures. He asked the Hasid about the circumstances of his going blind, and he told him. "There is no cure for you," said the man. "You have seen the original light, the light on the days of creation, which empowered the first people on earth to see from one end of the world to the other, which was hidden after their sinning, and is only revealed to *zaddikim* [holy men] in the Torah. Whoever beholds it unlawfully—his eyes will be darkened forever."

MARTIN BUBER

❖

[AFTER THE death of Rabbi Shimon bar Yochai,] Rabbi Chiyah . . . fasted for forty days so that he should be able to see Rabbi Shimon, but he was told, "You are not worthy to see him." He wept and then fasted for another forty days.

He was then shown a vision. He saw Rabbi Shimon and his son Eliezer studying a concept that he had discussed with Rabbi Yose. Many thousands were listening to his words.

At that moment, he saw many great lofty Wings. Rabbi Shimon and his son Eliezer mounted them, they ascended to the Academy of the Heavens. While they were there, the Wings waited for them.

He then saw [Rabbi Shimon and his son Eliezer] returning. They shone with a renewed glory, brighter than the sun.

Rabbi Shimon . . . said, "Let Rabbi Chiyah enter. Let him see to what extent the Blessed Holy One will renew the faces of the righteous in the World to Come. Happy is he who comes here without shame. Happy is he who can stand in this world like a mighty pillar."

[Rabbi Chiya then] saw [himself] enter. Rabbi Eliezer was standing, and all the others who were sitting there [stood up before Rabbi Chiyah]. He was very ashamed, but he entered, going to the side and sitting at the feet of Rabbi Shimon. . . .

[The Messiah] saw Rabbi Chiyah sitting at the feet of Rabbi Shimon. He said, "Who allowed a person wearing the clothing of the physical world to come here?"

Rabbi Shimon replied, "He is Rabbi Chiyah, the shining light of the Torah."

[The Messiah] said, "Let him and his sons die so that they can enter your academy."

Rabbi Shimon responded, "Let him be given more time [on earth]."

He was then given additional time. He left that place, trembling, with tears streaming from his eyes. Rabbi Chiyah trembled, wept and said, "Happy is the portion of the righteous in that world. And happy is the portion of the son of Yochai, who is worthy of all that."

ZOHAR (trans. Aryeh Kaplan)

◈

WHEN MOSES went up to heaven to receive the Bible he found the Holy One sitting and filling in little crowns over the letters of the Torah. Moses said to Him: "Master of the Universe, why is it necessary to add these crowns?" God replied: "At the end of several generations there will be a certain man called Akiva ben Joseph who will interpret each little extra decoration and learn many precepts from them." Moses said to Him: "Master of the Universe, show him to me." "Move backwards," said God. Moses went and sat at the back of Rabbi Akiva's class. He could not understand what they were being taught and his spirit sank. When they reached a certain issue Rabbi Akiva's pupils asked him: "Rabbi, how do we know this?" To which Rabbi Akiva replied: "This is a tradition which goes back to Moses at Sinai." On hearing this, Moses' spirit revived.

ALAN UNTERMAN

ECSTASY

YOU CAN shout loudly in a "small still voice." You can scream without anyone hearing you shouting with this soundless "small still voice."

Anyone can do this. Just imagine the sound of such a scream in your mind. Depict the shout in your imagination exactly as it would sound. Keep this up until you are literally screaming with this soundless "small still voice."

This is actually a scream and not mere imagination. Just as some vessels bring the sound from your lungs to your lips, others bring it to the brain. You can draw the sound through these nerves, literally bringing it into your head. When you do this, you are actually shouting inside your brain.

When you picture this scream in your mind, the sound actually rings inside your brain. You can stand in a crowded room, screaming in this manner, with no one hearing you.

Sometimes when you do this, some sound may escape your lips. The voice, traveling through the nerves, can also activate the vocal organs. They might then produce some sound, but it will be very faint.

It is much easier to shout this way without words. When you wish to express words, it is much more difficult to hold

the voice in the mind and not let any sound escape. But
without words it is much easier.

NACHMAN OF BRATZLAV (*trans. Aryeh Kaplan*)

❖

THINK OF yourself as nothing, and totally forget yourself
when you pray. Only have in mind that you are praying for
the Divine Presence.

You can then enter the Universe of Thought, a state that
is beyond time. Everything in this realm is the same, life
and death, land and sea. . . . But in order to enter the
Universe of Thought where all is the same, you must relin-
quish your ego, and forget all your troubles.

You cannot reach this level if you attach yourself to physical, worldly things. You are then attached to the division
between good and evil, which is included in the seven days
of creation. How then can you approach a level above time,
where absolute unity reigns?

Furthermore, if you consider yourself as "something,"
and ask for your own needs, God cannot clothe Himself in
you. God is infinite, and no vessel can hold Him at all,
except when a person makes himself like Nothing.

THE MAGGID OF MEZERITCH (*trans. Aryeh Kaplan*)

❖

IT WAS the custom of my teacher [Isaac Luria, the Ari],
of blessed memory, to kiss the scroll of the Torah and to
accompany it, walking behind it when it [was] brought from

the Ark to the Reader's table in order to be read. After this, he would remain there next to the table until they opened the Torah scroll and showed it to the congregation. . . . Then he would gaze upon the letters of the Torah. He used to say that a person could draw great light upon himself by looking at the Torah so closely that he was able to read the letters clearly. . . . Often my master used to pray in his own home with a quorum of ten individuals, on weekdays as well as on the Sabbath, without worrying about whether there was a Torah scroll available from which to read.

HAYIM VITAL (*trans. Lawrence Fine*)

❖

ONCE DURING the morning when Rabbi Schneur Zalman of Liadi was sitting drinking coffee, holding his glass in his hands, he talked about the holiness of his colleague Rabbi Zusya. "Master of the Universe," he said, "why is it that the Zaddik Rabbi Zusya, when he thinks about the divinity of even a small part of the universe, the awe of God falls on him, and his bowels give way from the great fear he feels, whereas I, who understand all the kabbalistic mysteries of the cosmos, nevertheless remain steady and do not tremble?" As he was speaking a great shaking and trembling overtook him, and the glass fell from his hand, his face started burning like fire, his eyes bulging; all this went on for about half an hour.

ALAN UNTERMAN

❖

A PERSON comes into a store where they sell many types of delicacies and sweetmeats. The first thing the storekeeper does is to give him a sample of each kind, in order that the customer should have an idea of what to buy. When he tastes it and sees how good it is, he wants to sample more. But the storekeeper then says, "You have to pay for anything you take. We do not give away anything free here."

The "free sample" is the Light that a person feels when he first begins to draw close [to God]. Through the taste of this Light, he can subjugate all evil, and return everything to the ultimate Good. This is [a "free sample"] given to the individual so that he should know the taste of serving God.

YITZCHAK ISAAC OF KAMARNA (*trans. Aryeh Kaplan*)

❖

BEFORE HE passed away [Rabbi Nachman] said, "I have already reached such a level that I can no longer advance while still clothed in this earthly body.

"I yearn to put this body aside, for I cannot remain on one level."

Although the rebbe attained the highest levels, he still strove to reach the next step. This was true throughout his life. He finally reached so high a level that he could no longer advance while still in a mortal body. He therefore had to leave this world.

NATHAN HERTZ OF NEMEROV (*trans. Aryeh Kaplan*)

❖

IT IS reported that Rabbi Zusya never taught Torah to his disciples around the Sabbath table, as was the general custom. The reason for this was that the pupils of the Maggid only used to teach what they had heard from their master around the Sabbath table, and this Rabbi Zusya could not do. For when the Maggid used to begin to teach he would open with a verse from Scripture which began with the words: "And God said," or, "And God spoke." When Rabbi Zusya heard these words from the mouth of the Maggid he would immediately feel a mystical illumination, and start moving to and fro. This caused a disturbance so they had to take him outside. He would stand in an outer room and climb up the walls shouting: "And God said," or, "And God spoke," in a loud voice. Only when the Maggid had finished his discourse would Rabbi Zusya calm down.

ALAN UNTERMAN

◈

A *zaddik* [holy man] told:

"In my youth I once attended a wedding to which the rabbi of Lublin had also been invited. Among the guests were more than two hundred *zaddikim,* as for the Hasidim—you could not even have counted them! They had rented a house with a great hall for the rabbi of Lublin, but he spent most of the time alone in a little room. Once a great number of Hasidim had gathered in the hall and I was with them. Then the rabbi entered, seated himself at a small table and sat there for a time in silence. Then he rose, looked around, and—over the heads of the others, pointed at me, standing up against the wall. 'That young man over there,' he said, 'shall light my pipe for me.' I made my way through the crowd, took the pipe from his hands, went to the kitchen, fetched a glowing coal, lit the pipe, brought it back into the hall, and handed it to him. At that moment I felt my senses taking leave of me. The next instant the rabbi began to speak and said a few words to me, and at once my senses returned. It was then that I received from him the gift of stripping myself of all that is bodily. Since then, I can do this whenever I want to."

MARTIN BUBER

❖

A PERSON who desires to gladden his soul ought to seclude himself for a portion of the day for the purpose of meditating upon the splendor of the letters YHVH. . . . When an individual meditates upon this name his soul lights up and shines wondrously. The soul becomes filled with happiness, and by virtue of the power of this illumination, it is invested with the strength with which to emit sparks. This joy extends even to the body . . . so that deceit is unable to govern it. Such is the status accorded the righteous who cleave to the name of God. For even in death the righteous are called "living." By virtue of their cleaving to the name YHVH—the wellspring of all life—they are invested with a degree of vitality.

ELIJAH DE VIDAS (trans. Lawrence Fine)

❖

YOUR LIFE blood is in your heart. . . . This blood within you will begin to vibrate because of the living permutations [of YHVH] that loosen it. Your entire body will then begin to tremble, and all your limbs will be seized with shuddering. You will experience the terror of God, and will be enveloped with fear of Him.

You will then feel as if an additional spirit is within you, arousing you and strengthening you, passing through your entire body and giving you pleasure. It will seem as if you have been annointed with perfumed oil, from head to foot.

You will rejoice and have great pleasure. You will experience ecstasy and trembling—ecstasy for the soul, and trembling for the body. This is like a rider who races a horse; the rider rejoices and is ecstatic, while the horse trembles under him. . . .

The Divine Presence will then rest on you, and the Fifty Gates of Understanding will be opened in your heart. From then on, you will realize Who is with you, Who is over your head, and Who is in your heart. You will then recognize the true way.

ABRAHAM ABULAFIA (*trans. Aryeh Kaplan*)

❖

ONCE, RABBI Dov Baer of Lubavitch, the son of Rabbi Schneur Zalman, was learning in his house and beside him was his daughter in a cradle. The child fell to the ground and lay there crying bitterly, but because of his deep concentration Rabbi Dov Baer heard nothing. His father, Rabbi

Schneur Zalman, who was learning in an attic room, came down, picked the child up and put it back in its cradle. "It's amazing to me," he said to his son, "that your mind is so constricted. When you are involved with something there is no room in your mind for anything else. I am not like that. When I am involved in deep contemplation I can still hear the noise of the fly crawling up the window pane."

ALAN UNTERMAN

Female Divinity

COME AND see:
The world above and the world below are perfectly
    balanced:
Israel below, the angels above.
Of the angels it is written:
"He makes His angels spirits" (Psalm 104:4).
But when they descend, they put on the garments of this
    world.
If they did not put on a garment befitting this world
they could not endure in this world
and the world could not endure them.

If this is so with the angels, how much more so with Torah
who created them and all the worlds
and for whose sake they all exist!
In descending to this world,
If She did not put on the garments of this world
the world could not endure. . . .

Come and see:
There is a garment visible to all.
When those fools see someone in a good-looking garment
they look no further.

But the essence of the garment is the body;
the essence of the body is the soul!

So it is with Torah.
She has a body:
the commandments of Torah,
called "the embodiment of Torah."

This body is clothed in garments:
the stories of this world.
Fools of the world look only at that garment, the story of
   Torah;
they know nothing more.
They do not look at what is under that garment.
Those who know more do not look at the garment
but rather at the body under that garment.
The wise ones, servants of the King on high,
those who stood at Mount Sinai,
look only at the soul, root of all, real Torah!
In the time to come
they are destined to look at the soul of the soul of Torah!

Come and see:
So it is above.
There is garment and body and soul and soul of soul.
The heavens and their host are the garment.
The Communion of Israel is the body
who receives the soul, the Beauty of Israel.
So She is the body of the soul.

The soul we have mentioned is the Beauty of Israel
who is real Torah.

The soul of the soul is the Holy Ancient One.
All is connected, this one to that one.

Woe to the wicked
who say that Torah is merely a story!
They look at this garment and no further.
Happy are the righteous
who look at Torah properly!

As wine must sit in a jar,
so Torah must sit in this garment.
So look only at what is under the garment!
So all those words and all those stories—
they are garments!

ZOHAR (*trans. Daniel Chanan Matt*)

❖

"I AM the Mother."

"I am the Mother who chastises."

"I am the Matrona."

"I am the redeeming angel."

"I am the emissary of the Holy One, blessed be he. . . . I
watch over you steadily. . . . The Shekhinah talks to you. . . .
Go to a pure place, thinking constantly of Torah without
letting your thoughts wander even for a second, even while
you are eating or talking. . . .

"Unify your heart constantly, at all times, at all hours, in all places, thinking of nothing except me, as I appear in my Torah and ritual. This is the mystery of unity, where a person yokes himself literally with his Creator. For the soul that attaches itself to Him, along with its body and limbs, literally becomes a 'Camp of the Shekhinah.'"

JOSEPH CARO (*trans. Aryeh Kaplan*)

◈

THE FEMININE principle . . . is . . . identified with the Divine Presence (Shekhinah), the essence of God that pervades all creation. It is this Essence that is the true beauty of all things. Thus, whenever one contemplates any beauty, he must realize that this is the Divine Essence, and can thus make use of it to begin the ascent on the Ladder.

Although the word *Nekevah* alludes to the orifices of a woman in the physical sense, it also refers to the spiritual orifices of Malkhut-Kingship. It is through these orifices that one can ascend into the spiritual realm. This is represented by the opening on the bottom of the letter *heh* [ה].

NEHUNIA BEN HAKANAH (*trans. Aryeh Kaplan*)

◈

[THE ARI] once said to [Abraham ben Eliezer ha-Levi]: "Now, know that your days are completed and that you have no longer to live unless you perform a certain act of restitution which I shall teach you. If you carry it out you may live another twenty-two years. This is what you must do: Travel to Jerusalem and go to the Western Wall where you should pour out your prayers and your tears; and if you are acceptable before your Maker you will merit a vision of the Shekhinah. Then you may rest assured that you will live an additional twenty-two years."

As soon as he heard this, the honored Rabbi Abraham ben Eliezer ha-Levi sold all the possessions in his house in order to pay his expenses for the journey and went to Jerusalem. He immediately secluded himself without interruption for three days and nights, which he spent in fasting, wearing sack cloth and in great weeping. After these three days he proceeded to the Western Wall where he began to pray and weep bitterly. While doing so he lifted up his eyes and saw upon the Wall the likeness of a woman with her back turned towards him. . . . As soon as he saw her he fell upon his face, crying out and weeping: "Mother, mother, mother of Zion, woe is me that I have seen you thus!" And he continued to weep bitterly, afflicting himself, tearing hair out of his beard and head until he fainted and fell deeply asleep.

Then in a dream he saw the Shekhinah coming towards him and, placing her hand upon his face, [she wiped] away the tears from his eyes. She said to him: "Console yourself, Abraham my son, for 'there is hope for thy future, saith the Lord, and your children shall return to their own border' [Jeremiah 31:17] 'for I will cause their captivity to return, and will have compassion upon them'" [Jeremiah 33:26].

Our honored Rabbi Abraham awakened from his sleep and returned to Safed, joyful and in high spirits. The Ari . . . said to him: "I can readily see that you have been privileged [with] a vision of the Shekhinah. From now on you may

rest assured that you will live another twenty-two years."
And so it came to pass.

HAYIM VITAL (trans. Lawrence Fine)

❖

THE SECRET of Sabbath:
She is Sabbath!
United in the secret of One
to draw down upon Her the secret of One.

The prayer for the entrances of Sabbath:
The holy Throne of Glory is united in the secret of One,
prepared for the High Holy King to rest upon Her.
When Sabbath enters She is alone,
separated from the Other Side,
all judgments removed from Her.
Basking in the oneness of holy light,
She is crowned over and over to face the Holy King.
All powers of wrath and masters of judgment flee from Her.
There is no power in all the worlds aside from Her.
Her face shines with a light from beyond;
She is crowned from below by the holy people,
and all of them are crowned with new souls. . . .
[They] bless Her with joy and beaming faces.

ZOHAR (trans. Daniel Chanan Matt)

❖

WHEN WE pray and say . . . "the great God," God clothes
himself with greatness. When we say, "the Mighty," God

clothes Himself with might. When we say, "the Fearsome,"
God clothes Himself with fearsomeness.

The attribute through which God clothes Himself
through our prayers is called "Mother."

LEVI YITZCHAK OF BERDICHOV (*trans. Aryeh Kaplan*)

❖

I SING in hymns
to enter the gates,
of the Field
of holy apples.

A new table
we prepare for Her,
a lovely candelabrum
sheds its light upon us.

Between right and left
the Bride approaches,
in holy jewels
and festive garments.

Her Husband embraces Her
in Her foundation,
giving Her pleasure,
squeezing out His strength.

Torment and trouble
are ended.

Now there are joyous faces
and spirits and souls.

He gives Her great joy
in twofold measure.
Light shines upon Her
and streams of blessing.

Bridesmen, go forth
and prepare the Bride's adornments,
food of various kinds
all manner of fish.

To beget souls
and new spirits
on the thirty-two paths
and three branches.

She has seventy crowns
and the supernal King,
that all may be crowned
in the Holy of Holies.

All the worlds are engraved
and concealed within Her,
but all shine forth
from the "Old of Days."

May it be His will
that He dwell among His people,

who take joy for His sake
with sweets and honey.

In the south I set
the hidden candelabrum,
I make room in the north
for the table with the loaves.

With wine in beakers
and boughs of myrtle
to fortify the Betrothed,
to strengthen the weak.

We plait them wreaths
of precious words
for the crowning of the seventy
in fifty gates.

Let the Shekhinah be adorned
by six Sabbath loaves
connected on every side
with the Heavenly Sanctuary.

Weakened and cast out
the impure powers,
the menacing demons
are now in fetters.

ISAAC LURIA (*trans. Lawrence Fine*)

They asked the Rabbi of Lublin: "Why is it that in the holy Book of Splendor, the turning to God which corresponds to the emanation 'understanding' [*binah*] is called 'Mother'?"

He explained: "When a man confesses and repents, when his heart accepts Understanding and is converted to it, he becomes like a newborn child, and his own turning to God is his mother."

MARTIN BUBER

❖

A KING once had a daughter who was good, pleasant, beautiful and perfect. He married her to a royal prince, and clothed, crowned and bejeweled her, giving her much money.

Is it possible for the king to ever leave his daughter? You will agree that it is not. Is it possible for him to be with her constantly? You will also agree that it is not. What can he then do? He can place a window between the two, and whenever the father needs the daughter, or the daughter needs the father, they can come together through the window.

It is thus written (Psalm 45:14), "All glorious is the king's daughter inside, her garment is interwoven with gold."

NEHUNIA BEN HAKANAH (*trans. Aryeh Kaplan*)

❖

SHEKHINAH DOES not reside except in a heart which is contrite. . . . A person must prepare a lovely dwelling place in his heart for the Shekhinah. This means that an individual has to act humbly and avoid losing his temper. For when he behaves in an arrogant manner, the Shekhinah takes flight and a handmaiden rules in her mistress' place. She will not abide with an individual who is not pleasing to the Holy One, blessed be He, and She will not glorify his soul in the world to come.

ELIJAH DE VIDAS (*trans. Lawrence Fine*)

The Seeker

THE HEBREW word for "wisdom" is *Chokhmah*. . . . This has the same letters as *Ko'ach Mah,* the "power" or "potential" of What. . . . Alternatively, *Ko'ach Mah* means "a certain potential." In the first sense, it is the power to question, to go beyond what is grasped with Understanding. In the alternate sense, it is an undefined potential, a potential that cannot be grasped with Understanding, which . . . must be experienced in its own right. As such, it is man's power to experience, since Wisdom is built out of experience. When

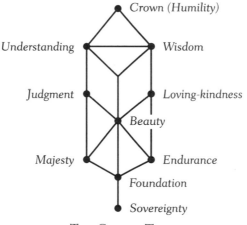

THE COSMIC TREE

one travels on the Paths of Wisdom, one begins with the Heart, which is Understanding. But then, one goes beyond this, to the Experience of Wisdom, which cannot be understood.

NEHUNIA BEN HAKANAH (trans. Aryeh Kaplan)

◇

IN THE days of the Great Maggid, a well-to-do merchant, who refused to have anything to do with Hasidic teachings, lived in Mezeritch. His wife took care of the shop. He himself spent only two hours a day in it. The rest of the time he sat over his books in the House of Study. One Friday morning, he saw two young men there whom he did not know. He asked them where they were from and why they had come, and was told they had journeyed a great distance to see and hear the Great Maggid. Then he decided that for once he too would go to his house. He did not want to sacrifice any of his study time for this, so he did not go to his shop on that day.

The maggid's radiant face affected him so strongly that from then on he went to his home more and more frequently and ended up attaching himself to him altogether. From this time on, he had one business failure after another until he was quite poor. He complained to the maggid that this had happened to him since he had become his disciple. The maggid answered: "You know what our sages say: 'He who wants to grow wise, let him go south; he who wants to grow rich, let him go north.' Now what shall one do who wants to grow both rich and wise?" The man did not know what to reply. The maggid continued: 'He who thinks nothing at all of himself, and makes himself nothing, grows spiritual, and spirit does not occupy space. He can be north and south at the same time." These words moved the merchant's heart and he cried out: "Then my fate is sealed!" "No, no," said the maggid. "You have already begun."

MARTIN BUBER

◇

[THE] PROPHET Elijah taught his disciples, "I call heaven and earth to witness, that any individual, man or woman, Jew or gentile, freeman or slave, can have Ruach ha-Kodesh (Holy Spirit) come upon him. It all depends on his deeds." . . . One must first repent every sin he has ever done, rectifying all the spiritual damage he has caused. He must then perfect his soul through keeping the positive commandments, as well as through complete concentration in prayer and diligent Torah study without ulterior motive. He must continue like an ox under its yoke, until the physical becomes weak. This should also include such disciplines as minimizing the amount of food one eats, waking up at midnight, shunning all unworthy traits, separating oneself from other people, and not speaking unnecessary words. One must also constantly purify his body through immersion in the *mikvah* [ritual bath].

After this, one should meditate . . . occasionally on the fear of God. He should mentally depict the letters of the Tetragrammaton. At this time, he should be careful to keep

his thoughts away from all worldly vanities, binding himself
to the love of God with great passion.

HAYIM VITAL (*trans. Aryeh Kaplan*)

◇

To NOURISH the spiritual center in the heart of the seeker
and to cultivate the first level of mystic consciousness,
members of the community of Safed followed a course of
instruction laid out by their teacher, Moses Cordovero. It
consisted of:

1. Forbearance in the face of insult
2. Patience in enduring evil
3. Pardon, to the point of erasing the evil suffered
4. Total identification with one's neighbor
5. Complete absence of anger, combined with appro-
   priate action
6. Mercy, to the point of recalling only the good qualities
   of one's tormentor
7. Eliminating all traces of vengefulness
8. Forgetting suffering inflicted on oneself by others and
   remembering the good
9. Compassion for the suffering without judging them
10. Truthfulness
11. Mercy beyond the letter of the Law with the good
12. Assisting the wicked to improve without judging them
13. Remembering all human beings always in the inno-
    cence of their infancy.

KABBALAH: THE WAY OF THE JEWISH MYSTIC

◈

THE HOLY Ari [Isaac Luria] said to Rabbi Moses Alshekh (who desired very much to study Kabbalah) that his soul had not come into the world for this, and that in a previous incarnation his soul had already learnt sufficient theosophic wisdom. But Rabbi Moses was very insistent so the Ari said to him: "I will give you a sign. Tomorrow, go to the place which I and my circle of mystics always pass by on our way to welcome the Sabbath. If you see us going along the road, know that I am only trying to test your perseverance. But if you do not see us know for sure that your soul did not come into this world to study kabbalistic wisdom." When Rabbi Moses heard this it seemed to him a very good idea, so around midday on Friday he put on his Sabbath clothes and sat by the roadside to wait for the Ari and his colleagues to pass. He remained waiting patiently for their coming, but just when the moment arrived he fell into a deep sleep. The Ari and his circle went by, and he did not see them. When the Ari's party were returning he told his disciples to awaken him, because the sun had already set. Rabbi Moses stood up in utter confusion: "What have I done? All day I was waiting and looking, and just at the crucial moment I fell asleep."

ALAN UNTERMAN

◈

IT HAS been taught:
When a human being is created,

on the day he comes into the world,
simultaneously, all the days of his life are arranged above.
One by one, they come flying down into the world
to alert that human being, day by day.
If, when a day comes to alert him,
he sins on that day before his Master,
then that day climbs up in shame,
bears witness, and stands alone outside.

It has been taught:
After standing alone
it sits and waits for that human to turn back to his Master,
to restore the day.
If he succeeds, that day returns to its place;
if not, that day comes down to join forces with the outlaw
    spirit.
It molds itself into an exact image of that human
and moves into his house to torment him.
Sometimes his stay is for the good
if one purifies himself.
If not, it is a horrible visitation.
Either way, such days are lacking, missing from the total.
Woe to the human being
who has decreased his days in the presence of the Holy
    King,
who has failed to reserve days up above—
days that could adorn him in that world,
days that could usher him in to the presence of the Holy
    King!

ZOHAR (*trans. Daniel Chanan Matt*)

❖

WHEN THE righteous man worships and studies Torah for
God's sake, he becomes like a magnet. He attracts all the
good portions and holy Sparks, wherever they are scattered
among the Outside Forces.

Each holy Spark is then lifted up from the lowest level.
It can raise itself from the Source of Good, and it is like a
person rescued from captivity and imprisonment. Up until
now, that holy Spark was locked up and imprisoned in a
lowly, evil place. . . .

A person can thus elevate such a holy Spark. That Spark
can then experience the highest pleasure, and it gives
thanks and praises the God of the Universe. All the Portions of good that escaped from the realm of evil also give
thanks and praise. . . .

When God sees the Portions of good and holiness that
are elevated from the hand of the Oppressors, He has the
greatest possible delight.

Through his worship and the light of his Torah study, the
righteous man returns all the holy Sparks to their Root in
good. Through this worship, where everything is brought
back to its Root and Source, the King of the Universe receives His desired delight from His handiwork.

THE OPTER REBBE (*trans. Aryeh Kaplan*)

❖

IN WHAT way should sacred books be treated? A person
ought to place his books in the most choice location in his

home and cover them with a prayer shawl. Just as we construct high shelves upon which to place food—in order to keep it from mice and cats—so one should also guard the honor belonging to God. When an individual transfers his books from one place to another, he should not treat them as he does other objects. Rather, he must move them in a dignified and respectful manner as one would carry the garments of a king in his presence. He should not touch them unless his hands are clean. These are acts of piety which are known only to oneself; a person who stands in awe of God will observe all of them.

ELIJAH DE VIDAS (*trans. Lawrence Fine*)

◇

MANY SAGES maintain that one who possesses all the necessary qualifications has methods through which he can . . . peek into chambers on high. One must first fast for a certain number of days. He then places his head between his knees, and whispers into the ground many songs and praises known from tradition. . . .

It is with regard to such an experience that the Talmud teaches, "Four entered the Orchard." The chambers are likened to an orchard and are given this name. . . .

It is taught that Ben Azzai gazed and died. This is because it was his time to leave the world.

It is also taught that Ben Zoma gazed and was stricken. This means that he became insane because of the confounding visions that his mind could not tolerate. . . .

When the Talmud states that the Other "cut his plantings," it is again using the allegory of the orchard. Since one of the four did irreparable damage, he is likened to one who enters an orchard and cuts down its trees. The Other assumed that there are two Authorities . . . as well as independent domains of good and evil, like light and darkness. . . .

Rabbi Akiva was the most perfect of them all. He gazed properly, not exceeding his limitations, and his mind was able to encompass these mighty confounding visions. God gave him power so that as long as he gazed he kept proper thoughts in his mind and maintained a proper mental state.

HAI GAON (*trans. Aryeh Kaplan*)

MEDITATION

You should be in a room by yourself, after immersion [in the ritual bath] and sanctification. It should be a place where you will not be distracted by the sound of human voices or the chirping of birds. The best time to do this is shortly after midnight.

Close your eyes and divest your thoughts of all worldly things. It should be as if your soul had left your body, and you should be as devoid of sensation as a corpse. Then strengthen yourself with a powerful yearning, meditating on the supernal universe. There you should attach yourself to the Root of your soul and to the Supernal Lights.

It should seem as if your soul had left your body and had ascended on high. Imagine yourself standing in the supernal universes . . . have in mind that . . . you are transmitting Light and Sustenance to all universes. . . .

Meditate . . . in thought for a short time, and attempt to sense if the Spirit . . . rested on you.

If you do not feel anything, it can be assumed that you are not fit and ready for it. You should therefore strengthen yourself all the more with worship and holiness. After a few days, you should meditate again in this manner, until you are worthy that the Spirit should rest upon you.

HAYIM VITAL *(trans. Aryeh Kaplan)*

❖

YOU SHOULD be consistent in your meditation, expressing your thoughts before God each day.

Even if you cannot speak at all, you should simply repeat a single word, and this, too, is very good. If you can say nothing else, remain firm, and repeat this word over and over again, countless times. You can spend many days with this one word alone, and this will be very beneficial. Remain firm, repeating your word or phrase countless times. God will eventually have mercy on you and will open your heart so that you will be able to express all your thoughts.

NACHMAN OF BRATZLAV (*trans. Aryeh Kaplan*)

❖

TAKE IN your hand a scribe's pen. Write speedily, letting your tongue utter the words with a pleasant melody, very slowly. Understand the words that leave your lips. The words can consist of anything that you desire, in any language that you desire, for you must return all languages to their original substance. . . .

Take the pen in your hand, like a spear in the hand of a warrior. When you think of something, uttering it in your heart with specific letters, also express it with your mouth. Listen carefully, and "watch what emanates from your lips" (Deuteronomy 23:24). Let your ears hear what your lips speak, and with your heart, understand the meaning of all these expressions.

Write each expression down immediately. Manipulate

the letters, and seek out other words having the same numerical value, even if they do not follow my path. . . .

You must be alone when you do this. Meditate . . . in a state of rapture so as to receive the divine influx, which will bring your mind from potential to action.

Permute the letters, back and forth, and in this manner, you will reach the first level. As a result of the activity and your concentration on the letters, your mind will become bound to them. The hairs on your head will stand on end and tremble.

ABRAHAM ABULAFIA (*trans. Aryeh Kaplan*)

❖

I HAD asked my master [the Ari, Isaac Luria] to teach me a Yichud [unification exercise] so that I should gain enlightenment. He replied that I was not ready. I continued to press him until he gave me a short Yichud, and I got up at midnight to make use of it.

I was immediately filled with emotion, and my entire body trembled. My head became heavy, my mind began to swim, and my mouth became crooked on one side. I immediately stopped meditating on that Yichud.

In the morning, my master saw me, and he said, "Did I not warn you? If not for the fact that you are a reincarnation of Rabbi Akiva, you would have [become insane] like Ben Zoma. There would have been no way to help you."

He then touched my lips, making use of a Kavanah [phrase of directed concentration] that he knew. He did this each morning for three days, and I was healed.

HAYIM VITAL (*trans. Aryeh Kaplan*)

❖

Rabbi Moses ben Nahman said: A person should keep God and His love in his consciousness at all times. He should not separate his thoughts from Him when he journeys on the way, nor when he lies down, nor when he rises up. Until he reaches the spiritual level at which when he speaks to people he speaks only with his mouth and tongue, but his consciousness is not with them—it is in the presence of God. It is possible for those who reach this spiritual level that whilst they are yet alive they are bound up in the bond of eternal life. For they themselves have become a dwelling place for God's divine Presence.

ALAN UNTERMAN

❖

Divesting oneself of the physical . . . means that the individual becomes totally unaware of his bodily feelings, and completely ceases to visualize this world. All that a person then visualizes are the universes on high, with their entire host of angels and archangels.

When a person then enters the Universe of Closeness . . . he feels nothing at all. He only experiences the most ethereal feeling, which is the closeness of God.

When an individual reaches this level, he can be aware of the future. One can know future events even in the lower universes, since they are announced by [angels called] Cherubim. . . .

When man nullifies himself completely and attaches his

thoughts to Nothingness, then a new sustenance flows to all universes. This is a sustenance that did not exist previously.

A person must fear God so much that his ego is totally nullified. Only then can he attach himself to Nothingness. Sustenance, filled with all good, then flows to all universes.

LEVI YITZCHAK OF BERDICHOV (*trans. Aryeh Kaplan*)

❖

A PERSON who desires to gladden his soul ought to seclude himself for a portion of the day for the purpose of

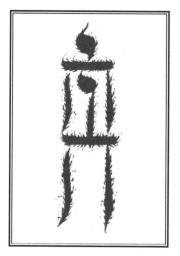

THE TETRAGRAMMATON, or YHVH [יהוה],
in a vertical arrangement representing the
Primordial Man, Adam Kadmon.

meditating upon the splendor of the letters YHVH. . . . For
our soul issues forth from the name YHVH. . . . Therefore,
when an individual meditates upon this name his soul
lights up and shines wondrously. The soul becomes filled
with happiness, and by virtue of the power of this illumination, it is invested with the strength with which to emit
sparks. This joy extends even to the body . . . so that deceit
is unable to govern it. Such is the status accorded the
righteous who cleave to the name of God. For even in death
the righteous are called "living." By virtue of their cleaving
to the name YHVH—the wellspring of all life—they are invested with a degree of vitality.

Another practice which facilitates cleaving to God consists in a person's secluding himself for part of the day while
he meditates upon the greatness of the Creator of all
things. . . . One should recite the final replies given to Job
by God, doing so out loud, with understanding and in a
pleasant manner. Similarly, one should recite several verses
from King David's Psalms, which tell of God's wonders and
greatness.

ELIJAH DE VIDAS (*trans. Lawrence Fine*)

❖

WITHOUT TELLING his teacher anything of what he was
doing, a disciple of Rabbi Barukh's [of Mezbizh] had inquired into the nature of God, and in his thinking had penetrated further and further until he was tangled in doubts,
and what had been certain up to this time, became uncer-
tain. When Rabbi Barukh noticed that the young man no

longer came to him as usual, he went to the city where he lived, entered his room unexpectedly, and said to him: "I know what is hidden in your heart. You have passed through the fifty gates of reason. You begin with a question and think, and think up an answer—and the first gate opens, and to a new question! And again you plumb it, find the solution, fling open the second gate—and look into a new question. On and on like this, deeper and deeper, until you have forced open the fiftieth gate. There you stare at a question whose answer no man has ever found, for if there were one who knew it, there would no longer be freedom of choice. But if you dare to probe still further, you plunge into the abyss." "So I should go back all the way, to the very beginning?" cried the disciple.

"If you turn, you will not be going back," said Rabbi Barukh. "You will be standing beyond the last gate: you will stand in faith."

MARTIN BUBER

❖

THE FOOD that comes from higher above is finer food,
coming from the sphere where Judgment is found.
This is the food that Israel ate when they went out of Egypt.
The food found by Israel that time in the desert,
from the higher sphere called Heaven—
it is an even finer food,
entering deepest of all into the soul,
detached from the body,
called "angel bread."

The highest food of all is the food of the Comrades,
those who engage Torah.
For they eat food of the spirit and the soul-breath;
they eat no food for the body at all.
Rather, from a high sphere, precious beyond all: Wisdom.

ZOHAR (*trans. Daniel Chanan Matt*)

HOLINESS

THE CREATOR is Himself, at one and the same time, knowledge, the knower, and the known. . . . There exists nothing which is not united to Him and which He does not find in His own essence. He is the type of all being, and all things exist in Him under their most pure and most perfect form.

MOSES CORDOVERO (*trans. Aryeh Kaplan*)

❖

SOMETIMES RABBI Abraham [son of the Maggid of Mezeritch] looked so great and awe-inspiring that men could not bear to look at him. One *zaddik*, who was performing some holy rite, did look at him and forgot whether or not he had said the blessing. On his return home, he refused both food and drink. Another martialed his courage four whole weeks, but when he crossed the threshold, and saw Rabbi Abraham binding on his phylacteries, he trembled and turned away, and did not again venture into his presence.

Barukh and Efraim, the grandsons of the Baal Shem Tov, once said to each other: "Why do you suppose people call the son of the maggid an angel? Let us have a look at him."

But when they reached the street in which he lived, and saw Rabbi Abraham's face in the window, they fled in such haste that Efraim dropped his book of psalms.

MARTIN BUBER

❖

FOR BEFORE the celestial world—known as the 377 compartments of the Holy One, blessed be He—was revealed; and before mist, electrum, curtain, throne, angel, seraph, wheel, animal, star, constellation, and firmament—the rectangle from which water springs—were made; and before the water, springs, lakes, rivers, and streams were created; and before the creation of animals, beasts, fowl, fish, creeping things, insects, reptiles, man, demons, specters, night demons, spirits, and all kinds of ethers—before all these things there was an ether, an essence from which sprang a primordial light refined from myriads of luminaries; a light, which, since it is the essence, is also called the Holy Spirit.

RABBI HAMAI (trans. Ronald C. Kiener)

❖

IF YOU wish to experience the Hidden Light and gain an awareness of the mysteries of the Torah that will ultimately be revealed, you should engage in much meditation directed toward God. Judge everything you do to see if it is worthy and proper to act in such a manner before God who is constantly doing good for you. You thus sustain your words with judgment. You are bringing yourself to judgment, and you yourself are the judge of all your deeds.

Through this, you can rid yourself of all fears. You will not be afraid of any official, lord, wild beast, robber, or anything else in the world. Your only fear will be an awe of God.

You will then be able to elevate fear to its root. . . . You will be worthy of perfect knowledge, and thus know whom you must really fear. You will realize that the only One you must fear is God, where your fear is a deep awe of His majesty.

Through this, you will be worthy of understanding the revealed, nonmystical elements of the Torah. You will also be worthy of true humility. You will then be able to pray with literal self-sacrifice, annulling everything physical and all ego during prayer. You will thus be able to pray without intent of gain, and will not think of the self at all. You will annul your physical being and your ego, and it will be just as if you do not exist.

Through this, you will then be worthy of comprehending the mysteries of the Torah. You will thus experience the Hidden Light, that will be revealed in the Ultimate Future.

NACHMAN OF BRATZLAV (*trans. Aryeh Kaplan*)

❖

WHEN HE heard of the great reputation of the holy Rabbi Israel Baal Shem Tov [also known as the Besht], and how everyone was journeying to him, Rabbi Dov Baer of Mezeritch, who was a scholar of considerable erudition, decided to visit him and test him. He wanted to know whether the Besht was really at such a high level or simply a charlatan. When he came to the Besht he thought he would at least hear some scholarly teaching; instead the Besht told him some stories. The same thing happened on the second day of his visit. The stories actually contained a wonderfully profound message, but Rabbi Dov Baer did not understand. Disappointed, he returned to his inn and prepared to return home. As he was about to leave the Besht sent for him. "Do you know how to explain kabbalistic teaching?" the Besht asked him. "Yes," he replied. So the former showed a certain passage in a mystical text to Rabbi Dov Baer, who contemplated it for a few moments and then explained it to the Besht. "I am afraid you really do not know anything," said the Besht. Rabbi Dov Baer looked at the passage again and said to the Besht: "That is the correct interpretation; if you know a better way of explaining it please tell me." The Besht started explaining the passage and as he did so the whole room was filled with light and a burning flame surrounded him, and they both saw that the angelic forces mentioned in the passage were present. "Your interpretation was the correct one," the Besht said, "but your way of studying lacked soul."

ALAN UNTERMAN

❖

GOD DESIRED to create the universe . . . for the sake of those who would do His will. . . . He therefore willed that He should constrict Himself into attributes and be given the title "First."

It is in this context that our sages call God "the Holy One." [The word *holy* has the connotation of "separation" and therefore, the appellation] "Holy One" means that God "separated" Himself (to the extent that we can express it) from His own infinite and boundless essence, in order to be called by various names, according to the devotion of those who do His will. As a result, He dwells among them, even in this physical world.

THE KOZNITZER MAGGID (*trans. Aryeh Kaplan*)

❖

EVEN THOUGH Scripture states that the Holy One, blessed be He, reveals himself in various manifestations, do not think that such is the case. Rather there are at His disposal fluctuating forces which change into various manifestations. These are the powers of angels. . . . But the Holy One, blessed be He, is one and utterly unchangeable. . . .

JACOB BEN JACOB HA-KOHEN (*trans. Ronald C. Kiener*)

❖

FOR MORE than fifty years, Elijah, the Gaon of Vilna, never slept more than half an hour at any one time during the night, nor did all the periods of his sleep total more than two hours. Even when he was weak and sick he never forsook his sacred studies. He would get up during the night in great awe, wash his hands, say the morning blessings with indescribable joy and love, and then stand on his feet from before midnight till dawn, a period of more than eight hours, studying with a voice both melodious and awesome. The sound of his voice burnt with a spiritual fire so that anyone who heard it was struck by soul-stirring feelings of holiness.

ALAN UNTERMAN

LOVE

ON ACCOUNT of his deep love for the Shekhina, a righteous person must bind himself to Her love, so much so that he will be jealous lest She separate from him and dwell with another. . . . Such a love involves rising at night in order to study Torah.

This kind of love may be compared to that of a man for his wife. For at night when he awakens with strong feelings of love, he will hasten to satisfy his longing with deep affection, particularly when he knows that she whom he loves, loves him as well. So it is with Torah scholars who are separated from their wives all week long because of their "marital" duty to the King's daughter, that is, the Torah.

ELIJAH DE VIDAS (*trans. Lawrence Fine*)

❖

HUMAN BEINGS are so confused in their minds!
They do not see the way of truth in Torah.
Torah calls out to them every day, in love,
but they do not want to turn their heads. . . .

To what can this be compared?
To a lovely princess,

beautiful in every way and hidden deep within her palace.
She has one lover, unknown to anyone; he is hidden too.
Out of his love for her, this lover passes by her gate
   constantly,
lifting his eyes to every side.
She knows that her lover is hovering about her gate
   constantly.
What does she do?
She opens a little window in her hidden palace
and reveals her face to her lover,
then swiftly withdraws, concealing herself.
No one near the lover sees or reflects,
only the lover, and his heart and his soul and everything
   within him
flow out to her.
And he knows that out of love for him
she revealed herself for that one moment
to awaken love in him.

ZOHAR (*trans. Daniel Chanan Matt*)

❖

IN ALL worldly delights, there is an element of the Highest
Love.

Through a person's natural desire for such delights, it
becomes easy for him to love God.

If this were not true, it would be very difficult even to
begin to love God. But when a person can arouse this love
through material delights, it becomes easy to love God. Understand this.

A person's love for material pleasures is a fallen love, but it is derived from the Highest Love. When he desires some worldly delight, he should realize that God is helping him, and making it easier for him to love God. God knows that without this, such love for God could not be aroused.

When one does not realize this, however, his worldly enjoyment causes this attribute of love to fall all the more.

Sometimes a person is aroused by an evil love. He desires to sin, but cannot act upon his evil thought because of some obstacle. This is also a result of God's help.

God sees that this person does not have enough wisdom to raise this fallen love up to its root and grasp onto the love of God. Rather, he wants to use it for evil. What God then does . . . is to constrict His glory still further, and bring about the obstacle. The individual is then at least "sitting and not doing."

NACHUM OF TCHERNOBLE (*trans. Aryeh Kaplan*)

◈

THE REWARD of an individual who serves God out of love consists in experiencing celestial joy of a wondrous character. . . . One who serves the King of the Universe out of love, without expectation of reward in this world or the next—but out of love alone—will be compensated by the Holy One, blessed be He, Himself. If he serves Him for the sake of some earthly reward, for the purpose of acquiring wealth or having children, he receives his reward entirely in this world. Just as this world is transitory, so too is his reward. And if he serves God for the sake of securing a

place in Paradise, his reward will be administered by the
angels who tend there. But, if he devotes himself to God
out of pure love, his soul cleaves to the "Infinite One." . . .
Those who attain the grade of super-soul are called God's
lovers.

ELIJAH DE VIDAS (*trans. Lawrence Fine*)

◇

WHILE OUTWARDLY the Song of Songs is simply a beautiful love song, it actually is the most profound song of unification of Z'er Anpin [the male face of God] and his Bride.
It thus contains a hidden holiness, just [as] this mundane
world contains the hidden holiness of the Shekhinah. Thus,
when one recites the Song of Songs and meditates on its
inner meaning, one can gain access to its inner essence, as
well as to the inner hidden essence of the mundane world,
which is the Shekhinah.

The Song of Songs is thus said to be the Holy of
Holies. . . . Similarly, when a person enters into a mystical
state, he is said to enter the realm of the "Holies. . . ." Thus,
when a person sanctifies himself and makes himself a re-
ceptacle for the Divine. . . . in a spiritual sense. . . . he is
also bound to it.

NEHUNIA BEN HAKANAH (*trans. Aryeh Kaplan*)

◇

THE MAN of true love is a very great man indeed, and
the very existence of time depends on him. For there is a

mountain and on this mountain is a stone from which a
spring flows. Now everything has a heart, including the
world itself whose heart is a fully developed structure with
face, hands, and feet, etc. But the toenail of the foot of the
heart of the world has more heart to it than the heart of any
other being. The mountain on which the stone and the
spring stand is at one end of the world and the heart of the
world is at the other end. The heart longs with an overpowering longing to come to the spring, and cries out because
of this longing. The spring too wants the heart. The heart
has two weaknesses. The first is that the sun pursues it and
burns it because it wants to draw near to the spring. The
second weakness is the great and overpowering desire
which it has to come to the spring, standing as it does on
the opposite side of the world. When the heart needs to
relax a little in order to regain its strength then a great bird
comes and spreads it wings over it, and protects it from the
sun's rays. Why then does the heart not go to the spring if
it longs for it so much? The reason is that if it wants to go
towards the mountain it cannot see the top of the mountain
and so loses sight of the spring, and not being able to see
the spring it would die. If the heart should perish then so
would the world, for it gives life to everything. So it cannot
move but stays where it is with its overpowering longing.
The spring has no time, for it is not within time at all. The
only time which the spring does have is what is given to it
as a present by the heart. This present consists only of one
day and were this day to draw to a close then the spring
would have no time and would disappear. If this happened
the heart too would be unable to continue to exist without

its beloved spring, and if the heart died so would the world. So when this day is drawing to a close the man of true love gives one day as a present to the heart, and the heart gives this day to the spring, so that the spring has time once again.

NACHMAN OF BRATZLAV (*trans. Alan Unterman*)

❖

WHEN A person wishes to unify the Blessed Holy One and His Divine Presence (the male and female aspects of the Divine), he must banish all other thoughts . . . regarding which it is written, "There are many thoughts in the heart of man" (Proverbs 19:21). One must then bring the Divine Presence into his mind, as the verse continues, "But the counsel of God will abide."

When a man comes together with his wife, he must remove all clothing, to be together with her as one, as it is written, "They shall be one flesh" (Genesis 2:21). In a similar manner, one must remove all other [thoughts, which serve as the soul's] garments, when he makes the Unification twice each day, declaring, "Hear O Israel, God is our Lord, God is One" (Deuteronomy 6:4).

TIKUNEY ZOHAR (*trans. Aryeh Kaplan*)

❖

WHEN THE Baal Shem Tov's wife died, it was obvious that he was suffering very greatly from the loss. It was not the way of the Baal Shem Tov to be concerned with worldly things, and the members of his household asked the reason for his anguish.

The Baal Shem replied that he [was] suffering because his mentality would have [to be buried and] lie in the ground. He said, "I was looking forward to rising in a flame. But now [without my wife], I am but half a body, and it is impossible. It is for this reason that I suffer so."

DOV BAER OF LINITZ (*trans. Aryeh Kaplan*)

❖

IN MY youth when I was fired with the love of God, I thought I would convert the whole world to God. But soon I discovered that it would be quite enough to convert the people who lived in my town, and I tried for a long time, but did not succeed. Then I realized that my program was still much too ambitious, and I concentrated on the persons in my own household. But I could not convert them either. Finally it dawned on me: I must work upon myself, so that I may give true service to God. But I did not accomplish even this.

HAYYIM OF ZANS (*trans. Martin Buber*)

❖

SOMETIMES YOU must worship in thought, with your soul alone.

Sometimes you can pray with love and awe and with great intensity without moving at all. Another person look-ing on can think that you are merely reciting the words without any feeling. For when you are very closely bound to God, you can serve Him with great love, with the soul alone.

This is the best type of worship. It moves quickly, and can bring you closer [to God] than prayer whose intensity is visible outside through your body. Such prayer is all inside, and therefore the Husks [evil] cannot grasp on to it. . . .

[A] person can read the Torah and see lights on the letters, even though he does not understand it fully. Since he is reading with great love and enthusiasm, God does not pay attention to the fact that he may not be reading correctly.

This is very much like a child who is very much loved by his parents. Even though it cannot speak well, its parents have great enjoyment when it asks for something.

The same is true when a person recites words of Torah with love [and devotion]. God has great delight, and does not pay attention to the fact that he does not read it correctly.

THE BAAL SHEM TOV (*trans. Aryeh Kaplan*)

CHARITY

A RICH man once came to the Maggid of Koznitz. "What are you in the habit of eating?" the maggid asked. "I am modest in my demands," the rich man replied. "Bread and salt, and a drink of water are all I need."

"What are you thinking of!" the rabbi reproved him. "You must eat roast meat and drink mead, like all rich people." And he did not let the man go until he had promised to do as he said.

Later the Hasidim asked him the reason for this odd request.

"Not until he eats meat," said the maggid, "will he realize that the poor man needs bread. As long as he himself eats bread, he will think the poor man can live on stones."

MARTIN BUBER

❖

AND WHAT is Loving-kindness? It is the Torah, as it is written: "All who are thirsty go to water" (Isaiah 55:1). And to him who does not have money, it is money, as it is written: "Go and take and eat, go and take it without money and without price, wine and milk." . . . He will feed you and teach you Torah for you already have become worthy

of it because of the merit of Abraham who used to do chari-
table deeds, and used to feed without pay and give drinks
of wine and milk free of charge.

What are wine and milk? And what is the connection
between them? This is to teach us that the wine is Fear,
and the milk is Loving-kindness.

NEHUNIA BEN HAKANAH (*trans. Ronald C. Kiener*)

❖

ANYONE WHO rejoices on the festivals
and does not give the Blessed Holy One His portion,
that stingy one with the evil eye,
Satan, Archenemy,
appears and accuses him,
removes him from the world.
Oh, how much trouble and suffering he brings upon him!

What is the portion of the Blessed Holy One?
To gladden the poor as best as one can.
For on these days
the Blessed Holy One comes to observe His broken vessels.
He enters from above
and if He sees that they have nothing to celebrate
He cries over them. . . .

The angels on high then declare:
"Master of the world!
Look at so-and-so who is eating and drinking his fill.
He could share something with the poor

but he gives them nothing at all!"
Then the Accuser steps forward, claims authority
and sets out in pursuit of that human being.

Who in the world was greater than Abraham?
He was kindhearted to all creatures.
One day he prepared a feast,
as it is written:
"The child grew up and was weaned,
and Abraham held a great feast on the day that Isaac was
    weaned"
    (Genesis 21:8)
To this feast Abraham invited all the great people of his
    time.

Now we have learned that the Accuser comes to every
    joyous meal
to see if the host has already provided for the poor
or invited the poor into his home.
If so, the Accuser departs and does not enter.
If not, he enters and witnesses this chaos of joy
without poor, without gifts for the poor.
Then he rises above and accuses the host.

When Abraham welcomed all those great people
the Accuser descended and stood at the door
disguised as a poor man.
But no one noticed him.
Abraham was serving the kings and celebrities. . . .

Meanwhile, the Accuser was still at the door. . . .
At once, the Accuser rose to face the Blessed Holy One.
He said, "Master of the world!
You call Abraham 'My friend'? (Isaiah 41:8)
He held a feast and gave nothing to me and nothing to the
    poor;
not even a single dove did he present to You!" . . .
The Blessed Holy One responded:
"Who in the world is like Abraham?"

But [Satan] held his ground until he ruined the whole
    celebration
and the Blessed Holy one commanded that Isaac be
    brought as an offering. . . .

All that suffering he brought about because [Abraham]
    gave nothing to the poor!

ZOHAR (*trans. Daniel Chanan Matt*)

❖

Even if a person is not perfect, there are some practices
that have the specific power to elevate his soul. . . . [One]
method involves giving charity properly. . . . This means
that he should not know to whom he is giving, and the
recipient should not know from whom he is receiving it.
It is also necessary that such charity be given to a proper
individual, one who is truly in need and worthy of it.

HAYIM VITAL (*trans. Aryeh Kaplan*)

❖

I HEARD in the name of Rabbi Yisroel Baal Shem Tov that if you do a good deed, but have an ulterior motive, it is better not to do it at all. The only exception is charity. Even though it is not as good as doing it with a pure motive, it is still a good deed, since you sustain the poor, no matter what your motive.

BINYAMIN OF ZLAZITZ *(trans. Aryeh Kaplan)*

❖

THE COMMANDMENTS constitute the King's ornaments with which He regales Himself; it is thus good for an individual to be filled with happiness while performing them, especially when he is aware of the restitution which he accomplishes through the enactment of a particular commandment, as well as the personal benefit he derives on his soul's behalf. Then he will experience even greater happiness. Particularly when it comes to the act of giving charity should an individual be joyful. For by doing so he cleaves to the Shekhinah, as Scripture says: "As for me, I shall behold Thy face in righteousness" [Psalm 17:15].

ELIJAH DE VIDAS *(trans. Lawrence Fine)*

❖

ONCE WHEN Rabbi Zusya was going around collecting money for the redemption of Jews taken captive, he came to an inn and saw a bird in a birdcage. "Here I am dragging my feet around collecting money for captives," he said, "but surely there is no greater redemption of captives than letting this bird go free." So he opened the cage and the bird flew off. When the landlord returned and found out what had happened he went up to Rabbi Zusya and said: "You madman, how could you do such a terrible thing? Do you know how much money it cost me?" And he beat Rabbi Zusya cruelly. Rabbi Zusya said to him: "I am going around to collect money to ransom people in need; you too will find yourself in need some day." Many years later the ex-landlord, now a poor man, came begging at Rabbi Zusya's door and told him how all his possessions had been destroyed in a fire and he was left with nothing.

ALAN UNTERMAN

❖

WHEN YOU discuss Godliness with a friend, the information that he receives from you is Direct Light. What you gain [from your own words] through him is Reflected Light.

Sometimes you can speak to a person about Godliness, and your words are not accepted. Still, you yourself can be motivated by your own words. Your words can literally bounce off from your friend, and be reflected back to you.

This is very much like a rubber ball. The reason a ball bounces back from a stone wall is because it cannot penetrate it. Similarly, when the other person refuses to accept what you tell him, your words are reflected back to you. You yourself are then influenced by your own words.

These same words may not have had any effect at all on

you if you had spoken them to yourself. But when you express them to someone else, and he is not influenced, they are reflected to you. You can then be motivated by your own words.

NACHMAN OF BRATZLAV (*trans. Aryeh Kaplan*)

◈

IN THE days of the Baal Shem, a rich and hospitable man lived in a nearby city. To every poor wayfarer, he gave food and drink and money to boot. But he felt the urgent need to hear words of praise from everyone he received into his house, and if such words did not come spontaneously, he threw out a deft phrase as bait, and then a big or little praise-fish was always sure to bite.

Once the Baal Shem sent one of his disciples, Rabbi Wolf Kitzes, cross-country, and told him to visit that rich man in the course of his journey. He was lavishly entertained and presented with a generous gift, but gave only sparse words of thanks. Finally his host said: "Don't you think that this is the proper way to practice hospitality?"

"We shall see," answered Rabbi Wolf. And not another word could the rich man get out of him. At nightfall, the host lay down among his guests according to his custom, for before falling asleep he liked to chat with them and hear something pleasing to his person. Just as he was dozing off, Rabbi Wolf touched him on the shoulder with his little finger. In his dream the man thought he was called to the king and had tea with him. But suddenly the king fell and was dead and they accused him of poisoning him and put him in jail. A fire broke out in the jail and he escaped and fled until he was far away. Then he became a water-carrier, but that was hard work and got him a meager living, so he moved to another region where water was scarce. But there they had a law that you were not paid unless the pail was full to the brim, and to walk with a full pail and never spill a drop was a difficult matter. Once when he was walking carefully, slow step by step, he fell and broke both legs, and there he lay and thought of his former life, and was amazed and wept. Then Rabbi Wolf touched him on the shoulder again with his little finger, and the man woke up and said: "Take me with you to your master."

The Baal Shem received the rich man with a smile. "Would you like to know where all that hospitality of yours has gone to?" he asked. "It has all gone into a dog's mouth."

The man's heart awoke and turned to God, and the Baal Shem instructed him how to lift up his soul.

MARTIN BUBER

◇

RABBI JACOB Yitzhak [of Lublin] was in the habit of taking poor wayfarers into his house and waiting on them himself. Once he had served such a man with food, filled his glass, and stood beside his chair ready to fetch him whatever he needed. After the meal, he took away the empty plates and platters and carried them into the kitchen. Then his guest asked him: "Master, will you tell me something? I know that you, in serving me, have fulfilled the command of God, who wishes the beggar to be honored as his envoy. But why have you taken the trouble to carry out the empty dishes?"

The rabbi replied: "Is not the carrying out of the spoon and the coal-pan from the Holy of Holies part of the service of the high priest, on the Day of Atonement!"

MARTIN BUBER

Daily Life

THE WORLD is full of strife.

There are wars between the great world powers.

There are conflicts within different localities.

There are feuds among families.

There is discord between neighbors.

There is friction within a household, between man and wife, between parents and children.

Life is short. People die every day. The day that has passed will never return, and death comes closer every day.

But people still fight and never once remember their goal in life.

All strife is identical.

The friction within a family is a counterpart of the wars between nations.

Each person in a household is the counterpart of a world power, and their quarrels are the wars between those powers. The traits of each nation are also reflected in these individuals. Some nations are known for anger, others for blood-thirstiness. Each one has its particular trait.

The counterparts of these traits are found in each household.

83

You may wish to live in peace. You have no desire for strife. Still you are forced into dispute and conflict.

Nations are the same.

A nation may desire peace and make many concessions to achieve it. But no matter how much it tries to remain neutral, it can still be caught up in war. Two opposing sides can demand its allegiance until it is drawn into war against its will.

The same is true in a household.

Man is a miniature world.

His essence contains the world and everything in it. A man and his family contain the nations of the world, including all their battles.

A man living alone can become insane.

Within him are all the warring nations.

His personality is that of the victorious nation.

Each time a different nation is victorious, he must change completely, and this can drive him insane. He is alone and cannot express the war within him.

But when one lives with others, these battles are expressed toward his family and friends.

NACHMAN OF BRATZLAV (*trans. Aryeh Kaplan*)

◇

DOV BAER, the Maggid of Mezeritch, said to his disciple the holy Rabbi Zusya of Hanipoli that in the service of God he should learn three things from a child and seven things

from a thief. From a child he should learn (1) always to be
happy; (2) never to sit idle; (3) to cry for everything one
wants. From a thief he should learn (1) to work at night; (2)
if one cannot gain what one wants in one night to try again
the next night; (3) to love one's co-workers just as thieves
love each other; (4) to be willing to risk one's life even for a
little thing; (5) not to attach too much value to things, even
though one has risked one's life for them, just as a thief will
resell a stolen article at a fraction of its real value; (6) to
withstand all kinds of beatings and tortures but to remain
what you are; (7) to believe that your work is worthwhile,
and not to be willing to change it.

ALAN UNTERMAN

❖

THE BLESSED Holy One does not place His abode
in any place where male and female are not found together.
Blessings are found only in a place where male and female
    are found, as it is written:
"He blessed them and called their name Adam
on the day they were created."
It is not written:
"He blessed him and called his name Adam."
A human being is only called Adam
when male and female are as one.

ZOHAR (trans. Daniel Chanan Matt)

❖

IT IS very good to have a special room, set aside for Torah study and prayer. Such a room is especially beneficial for secluded meditation and conversation with God. . . . It is very good even to sit in such a special room. The atmosphere itself is beneficial, even if you sit there and do nothing. . . . You can create your own "special room" under your Tallit [prayer shawl]. Just drape your Tallit over your eyes and express your thoughts to God as you desire.

You can also meditate with God in bed under the covers. . . . You can also converse with God while sitting before an open book. Let others think that you are merely [reading or] studying.

NACHMAN OF BRATZLAV (*trans. Aryeh Kaplan*)

❖

IN ROPTCHITZ, the town where Rabbi Naftali lived, it was the custom for the rich people whose houses stood isolated or at the far end of the town to hire men to watch over their property by night. Late one evening when Rabbi Naftali was skirting the woods which circled the city, he met such a watchman walking up and down. "For whom are you working?" he asked. The man told him and then inquired in his turn: "And whom are you working for, Rabbi?"

The words struck the *zaddik* [holy man] like a shaft. "I am not working for anybody just yet," he barely managed to say. Then he walked up and down beside the man for a long time. "Will you be my servant?" he finally asked. "I should like to," the man replied, "but what would be my duties?" "To remind me," said Rabbi Naftali.

MARTIN BUBER

◇

ONCE WHEN the Master, the holy Ari [Isaac Luria], was sitting in the house of study with his disciples he looked at one of them and said to him, "Go out from here, for today you are excommunicated from heaven." The disciple fell at the feet of the Master and said to him, "What is my sin? I will repent for it." So the Master said to him: "It is because of the chickens you have at home. You have not fed them for two days, and they cry out to God in their hunger. God will forgive you on condition you see to it that before you leave for prayers in the morning you give food to your chickens. For they are dumb animals and they cannot ask for their food."

ALAN UNTERMAN

◇

[CONCENTRATING] AND recalling every sin that one has done the entire day . . . should be done when the individual is lying in bed. All of his sins should be before his eyes, and he should repent them all. After saying the bedtime Shema, he should also confess them verbally. . . .

It is important not to omit even a single sin or fine point that one transgressed on that particular day. When going to sleep, he should confess them all [before God] and not forget even a single one. It appears that I heard from my master [Isaac Luria], however, that it is not necessary to review all that one had done that day, since this would be an endless task. But one must strive to do so, setting his heart to remember all that he had done wrong that day. This is sufficient.

HAYIM VITAL (*trans. Aryeh Kaplan*)

❖

ELIJAH, THE Gaon of Vilna, once asked his friend the Maggid of Dubno to give him ethical instruction so that he might strengthen himself in the service of God. Now the Gaon was known as a man of saintly disposition who spent all his waking time secluded in his room in study, prayer and contemplation. So the Maggid of Dubno said to him: "It is easy to be a *gaon* (sage) and a saint cloistered here in your room. You should go out into the marketplace and try to be a saint there."

ALAN UNTERMAN

❖

THE ESSENTIAL root principle of the Hasidic teaching of the Besht [Baal Shem Tov] is that a man should always remember that he has a duty to serve God at every moment, whether at the time that he is studying Torah, or praying, or performing some mundane physical activity, or occupied with worldly matters, or just having an ordinary conversation. Before him is always an element of good and an element of bad, and he needs to isolate the bad aspect and reject it, whilst isolating and strengthening the good element. In this way he serves God always, and it is as if he was engaged in the continual study of Torah even though he is walking about the marketplace.

ALAN UNTERMAN

GOOD AND EVIL

THERE WAS a road that went through the forest, passing a den of robbers, and it was very dangerous to anyone who would take it. Two people once took this road. One was insensibly drunk, while the other was sober.

The two men were waylaid by the robbers, and were robbed, beaten, and wounded, barely escaping with their lives. After they reached the end of the forest, they met a number of people.

Some people asked the drunk, "Did you pass through the forest in peace?" He replied, "It was peaceful; there is no danger at all." They then asked him about his bruises and wounds, and he did not know how to reply.

Other people raised the same question with the sober man. He replied, "Heaven forbid! You must be very careful, for the woods are full of fierce robbers." Speaking at great length, he warned them of the danger.

This is the difference. A wise man knows how to warn others, so that they know not to go through the dangerous place, unless they move swiftly and are well armed. The drunkard, on the other hand, does not know how to warn the others at all.

The righteous man who serves God [is like the wise man]. He is fully aware of the battle waged by the Evil

Urge, the robber lying on the path leading to the worship of God. He is aware of the danger, and is constantly alert to avoid a trap. He also knows how to warn others of the danger of these robbers. It is thus written, "The more knowledge, the more pain" (Ecclesiastes 1:18).

The wicked man, however, [is like the drunkard]. He constantly enjoys the snares of the Evil Urge, and says, "I am at peace—there is no danger in this world."

THE BAAL SHEM TOV (*trans. Aryeh Kaplan*)

❖

AT THE time when the Holy One created the world and wanted to reveal deep matters from their hidden recesses, and light from within darkness, they were intertwined with one another. Because of this, that out of darkness came light and from out of the hidden recesses were revealed deep matters, that one came from the other, it also is the other way around: out of the good emerges evil, and out of love emerges strict justice, since they are intertwined.

ZOHAR (*trans. Alan Unterman*)

❖

WHAT DOES the Evil Urge gain?

What is this like? A king appointed clerks over the lands of his kingdom, over his work and over his merchandise. Each and every thing had its clerk. There was one clerk in charge of the storehouse containing good food. Another was in charge of the storehouse containing stones. Every-

one came to the storehouse containing good food. The clerk
in charge of the storehouse of stones came and saw that
people were only buying from the other [clerk].

What did he do? He sent his messengers to tear down
the weak houses [so that people would need stones to rebuild them].

They could not do so, however, to the strong ones. He
said, "In the time that it takes to tear down one strong
[house], you can tear down ten weak ones. People will then
all come and buy stones from me, and I will not be inferior
to the other."

NEHUNIA BEN HAKANAH *(trans. Aryeh Kaplan)*

◇

[THE] FIRST man . . . was not the child of any woman but
was created from a pure and pristine likeness [of God],
lacking any evil inclination to sin. God commanded him
and warned him to keep one commandment for his own
benefit so that he could enjoy everlasting life. But he transgressed this first commandment.

We believe that the Creator did not want him to sin, nor
did He decree that he should. He simply commanded the
good. This is the case with other people and pious individuals. The patriarchs serve as an example—from them came
Esau and Ishmael and Hezekiah and Manasseh and many
other [sinners]. From the good came forth evil, and God
neither commanded nor demanded it. All this falls under
the category of silence: do not dwell on it—it is so awesome

that you ought not inquire, so hidden that you ought not pursue it.

ISAAC BEN JACOB HA-KOHEN (*trans. Ronald C. Kiener*)

◈

RABBI NACHMAN taught: It is known that the Sitra Ahra (literally "Other Side," i.e., evil) surrounds holiness. In particular a person who is drawn after sin is drawn after the Sitra Ahra; his place is there and the evil surrounds him on all sides. When his spirit revives and he wants to repent, he finds it very difficult to pray and to speak to God; his words and prayers are unable to pierce the barriers and screens which surround him and to rise up. They linger on his side of the barrier. When, however, he repents truly then his illuminated words split through the barriers and they take with them all his previous efforts at speech and prayer which have remained behind until now. How does one become worthy of being able to do this? The main thing is truthfulness, for everything depends on truth, and one must follow the truth according to the level that one is on. As the rabbis teach: The seal of God is truth.

ALAN UNTERMAN

◈

AFTER A person's death, his soul cleaves to one realm or another in accordance with his actions in this world. For a man is composed of both good and evil, that is, the good inclination and the evil inclination. If he subdues his evil inclination, he subjugates the forces of strictness and evil, and enables goodness to descend upon him. An individual must strengthen the good inclination so that it prevails over the evil inclination. And if, heaven forbid, he does the reverse, he injures the supernal roots and prevents blessing and divine abundance from flowing into this world. Therefore, he must always stand in awe of heaven lest he injure himself, that is, his soul, depriving it of its supernal light.

The husk, deriving from the realm of evil, is like the shell of a nut. The good element—which is concealed—is the kernel of the nut. Therefore, in order to achieve the fear of God—which is the good that is concealed—one must break and destroy one's evil obstinacy and distance himself from this quality to such a degree that he will be loathe to draw near to it again. Just as one must crack the shell of the nut in order to consume the wholesome kernel, and just as the nut possesses three layers of shells, so must one distance himself from three husks. The first of these is pride, for this is the root of all evil qualities. Second, corresponding to the nut's hard shell, is a man's stubbornness. The third is an angry person's fury and harsh words which make him seethe with the fire of the evil impulse and lead him to sin. When a man separates himself from the pleasures of this world, all of which derive from the husks, the serpent's skin, and the evil inclination, this realm is subdued. The same holds true when he is careful to avoid transgressing the Torah's negative commandments. For anyone who violates the negative commandments enables the evil serpent to penetrate the realm of holiness.

ELIJAH DE VIDAS (*trans. Lawrence Fine*)

◈

[THE] BLESSED Holy One has an Attribute whose name is Evil. . . .

It is the Form of a Hand.

It has many messengers, and the name of them all is Evil. Some of them are great, and some are small, but they all bring guilt to the world. . . .

Chaos . . . is nothing other than Evil. It confounds . . . the world and causes people to sin.

Every Evil Urge . . . that exists in man comes from there. . . . "If you listen to the voice of the Lord your God, and do what is upright in His eyes, and give ear to His commandments"—and not to the commandments of the Evil Urge— "and keep all His decrees"—and not the decrees of the Evil Urge—"[then all the sickness that I brought upon the Egyptians, I will not bring upon you,] for I am the God who heals you."

NEHUNIA BEN HAKANAH (*trans. Aryeh Kaplan*)

◈

RABBI YOSE said:
"When a person sees that evil imaginings are assailing him
    he should occupy himself with Torah and they will pass
    away."

Rabbi El'azar said:
"When that evil side approaches to seduce a human being
he should pull it toward Torah

and it will leave him.

Come and see what we have learned:

When that evil side confronts the Blessed Holy One,

accusing the world of evil doings,

the Blessed Holy One feels compassion for the world

and offers a device to human beings to save themselves
    from him,

to neutralize his power over them and their actions.

What is the device?

Engaging in Torah!" . . .

Rabbi Isaac said:

"The righteous are destined to see the Deviser of Evil in
    the shape of a huge mountain.

Astounded, they will say:

'How were we able to overturn that huge mountain?'

The wicked are destined to see the Deviser of Evil as thin
    as a thread of hair.

Astounded, they will say:

'How could we fail to overcome a thread of hair so thin?'

These will cry and those will cry.

The Blessed Holy One will sweep the Deviser of Evil off
    the earth

and slaughter him before their eyes,

and his power will be no more.

Seeing this, the righteous will rejoice,

as it is said:

'Surely the righteous will praise Your Name;

the upright will dwell in Your Presence'" (Psalms 140:14).

ZOHAR (trans. Daniel Chanan Matt)

◈

THE EVIL One is like a prankster running through a crowd, holding up his tightly closed hand. No one knows what he is holding, and he goes up to each individual and asks, "What do you suppose I have in my hand?"

Each one imagines that the closed hand contains just what he desires. They all hurry and run after the prankster. Then, when he has tricked them all into following him, he opens his hand and it is completely empty.

The same is true of the Evil One. He fools the world, tricking everyone into following him. All men think that his hand contains what they desire. But in the end, when he opens his hand, there is nothing in it. No worldly desire is ever fulfilled.

Worldly desires are like sunbeams in a dark room. They may seem solid, but the person who tries to grasp a sunbeam finds nothing in his hand. The same is true of all worldly desires.

NACHMAN OF BRATZLAV (*trans. Aryeh Kaplan*)

Community

WE SAY in our prayers, "Our God, and God of our fathers."

The reason for this is that there are two types of people who believe in God. The first one believes because he follows the ways of his fathers, strongly maintaining their tradition of faith. The second is the one who gains his faith through reason and philosophical thought.

There is an important difference between these two individuals.

The first one has the advantage that he cannot be tempted, even if he is confronted with philosophical proofs that might contradict his faith. His faith remains strong because of the traditions that he has from his fathers. Besides this, he has never depended on philosophical speculation.

On the other hand, this person also has a disadvantage. His faith is not well reasoned, nor thought out, and is essentially the result of habit.

The second one also has an advantage. He has discovered God with his logic, and is very strong in his faith. . . .

This one, however, also has a disadvantage. He can be persuaded by logic, and if confronted with proofs that tear down the logical structure [of his faith] he can be tempted away.

The person who gains his faith in both these ways has every advantage. He depends strongly on the traditions of his forefathers, while at the same time taking advantage of his logic in thinking things out. He thus has the best and most perfect faith.

THE BAAL SHEM TOV (*trans. Aryeh Kaplan*)

❖

As RABBI Abba has said:
"All those Comrades who do not love one another
pass away from the world before their time.
All the Comrades in the days of Rabbi Shim'on
shared a vital, spiritual love.
That is why Torah was revealed in the generation of Rabbi
    Shim'on."

As Rabbi Shim'on used to say:
"All Comrades who do not love one another
divert [themselves] from the straight path.
Moreover, they produce a defect in her!
For Torah embodies love, friendship, and truth:
Abraham loves Isaac; Isaac, Abraham;
they embrace one another.
Jacob is held by both of them in brotherhood and love.
They offer to one another their spirit, their breath of life!
Comrades must be just like that and not produce a defect!"

ZOHAR (*trans. Daniel Chanan Matt*)

◈

[Isaac Luria's] father died while he was still a child. Because of poverty, he went to Egypt, where he lived with his wealthy uncle. His brilliance continued to shine in dialectic . . . and logic.

By the time he was fifteen, his expertise in Talmud had overwhelmed all the sages in Egypt. At this time he married his uncle's daughter.

After he was married, he spent seven years meditating . . . with his master, Rabbi Betzalel Ashkenazi. He then meditated alone for six years.

He then added to this, meditating and reaching higher levels of holiness. This he did for two years straight, in a house near the Nile. There he would remain alone, utterly isolated, not speaking to any human being.

The only time he would return home would be on the eve of the Sabbath, just before dark. But even at home, he would not speak to anyone, even to his wife. When it was absolutely necessary for him to say something, he would say it in the least possible number of words, and then, he would speak only in the Holy Tongue (Hebrew).

He progressed in this manner and was worthy of [Divine Grace]. At times, Elijah revealed himself and taught him the mysteries of the Torah.

He was also worthy for his soul to ascend every night, and troops of angels would greet him to safeguard his way, bringing him to the heavenly academies. These angels would ask him which academy he chose to visit. Sometimes it would be that of Rabbi Shimon bar Yochai, and other times he would visit the academies of Rabbi Akiva or Rabbi Eliezer the Great. On occasion he would also visit the academies of the ancient Prophets.

HAYIM VITAL (*trans. Aryeh Kaplan*)

❖

ONE DAY, a Friday, the Ari [Isaac Luria] went out with his colleagues, as was his custom, to welcome the onset of the Sabbath in the fields outside Safed. He said to his associates: "Let us now go to Jerusalem, and let us rebuild the Temple, for I see that this moment is the End of Days leading to Redemption." Some of those present said: "How can we go to Jerusalem at just this moment seeing that it is many miles away?" Others of his circle said: "It is good, and we are ready to go. But first let us return and tell our wives so that they will not worry about us, and then we shall go." Then the Ari cried out with tears welling up in his eyes, and said to the members of his association: "I call heaven and earth to bear witness that from the time of Rabbi Simeon bar Yohai to this moment there was no more fitting hour for redemption than now. If you had agreed to this then the Temple would have been rebuilt and the scattered ones of Israel gathered in to Jerusalem. But now the moment has passed, and Israel has reentered exile anew."

ALAN UNTERMAN

❖

RABBI ELIMELEKH once set out for home from a city he had visited and all the Hasidim accompanied him for a long stretch of the way. When his carriage drove through the gate, he got out, told the coachman to drive on, and walked behind the carriage in the midst of the throng. The astonished Hasidim asked him why he had done this. He answered: "When I saw the great devotion with which you were performing the good work of accompanying me, I could not bear to be excluded from it!"

MARTIN BUBER

❖

RABBI ISHMAEL said: "I stood up and gathered the entire Great Tribunal (Sanhedrin) and the Lesser Tribunal, bringing them to the great third hall of the House of God. I sat on a couch of pure marble, given to me by my father Elisha. . . .

"Those who came included Rabban Shimon ben Gamaliel, Rabbi Eliezer the Great, Rabbi Eleazar ben Dama, Rabbi Eliezer ben Shamua, Rabbi Yochanan ben Dahavai, Rabbi Chananya ben Chanikai, Rabbi Jonathan ben Uziel, Rabbi Akiva, and Rabbi Yehuda ben Bava. We all came and sat before [Rabbi Nehunia ben Hakana]. The throngs of our companions stood on their feet, for they saw rivers of fire and brilliant flames separating them from us.

"Rabbi Nehunia ben Hakana sat and explained everything involving the Merkava [Heavenly Chariot]. He described its descent and ascent; how one who descends must descend, and how one who ascends must ascend."

THE GREATER HEKHALOTH (trans. Aryeh Kaplan)

❖

THE "CONGREGATION of Israel" refers to the souls of Israel, both past and future. Although they frequently intervene for mankind, they do not do so when man sins. This is related to the teaching that God consulted with the souls of the righteous at the time of creation.

NEHUNIA BEN HAKANAH (*trans. Aryeh Kaplan*)

DEATH

IMAGINE THAT you are in the middle of the sea, with a storm raging to the very heart of the heavens. You are hanging on by a hairbreadth, not knowing what to do. You do not even have time to cry out. You can only lift your eyes and heart to [God].

You should always lift your heart to [God] like this. Seclude yourself and cry out to [God]. The danger is more than imaginary. As you know deep down in your soul, every man is in great danger in this world.

Understand these words well.

NACHMAN OF BRATZLAV (*trans. Aryeh Kaplan*)

❖

RABBI ELIAHU di Vidas told me that he . . . asked my master [the Ari, Isaac Luria] this question, "How did earlier generations make use of the Divine Names?" He replied that one may use them if he can fulfil in himself the verse, "Maidens (*alamot*) love you" (Song of Songs 1:3). The Talmud says, do not read *alamot* (maidens), but *al mot* (over death), [making the verse read, "The one over death loves you."] This means that one must be so righteous that he is even loved by the Angel of Death.

If a person does not have any sin, the Accuser cannot come before the Blessed Holy One and say, "Behold this person is making use of Your Names, and on that day, he committed such a sin." [When such an accusation is made] that person is punished from heaven for making use of God's Names. But if he is totally without sin, then there is no way in which he can be denounced. The Angel of Death [who is identified with the Accuser] becomes his friend. Such a person can make use of Divine Names and not be punished. . . .

When a saint dies, he causes all the universes to unite. But there are saints who knew how to use Yichudim [Hebrew letter permutations] at auspicious times, and they could do this even during their lifetime. What other saints could accomplish only after death, they could do while they were still alive.

One such saint was Benaiah ben Yehoiada. It is for this reason that he was called "son of a Living Man" (2 Samuel 23:20), even after his death. . . .

There were other saints who resembled him in this respect. They included Moses, Rabbi Hamnuna the Elder, Rabbi Yebi the Elder, and others like them.

These saints were worthy of a very high level during their lifetime. Therefore, even after they died, whenever they see sages studying the Torah and meditating on higher Yichudim, they join them and reveal themselves. Sometimes they are there, but they remain concealed.

HAYIM VITAL (*trans. Aryeh Kaplan*)

❖

Once Rabbi Zusya prayed that he should be able to achieve the great awe of God which the angels have. He acquired such a tremendous sense of fear and awe that he was unable to stand or sit for even one moment. He hid himself, now under the bed, now in the dark corners of the house, and was unable to bear the great awe so that he almost died. He prayed to God that he should be a man once again. He said afterwards that man in his physical form is unable to attain this level.

ALAN UNTERMAN

❖

The first mention of death in the Torah is in relation to the Tree of Knowledge, where God tells Adam, "And from the Tree of Knowledge of Good and Evil, do not eat from it, for on the day you eat from it, you will be bound to die" (Genesis 2:17). Hence, on the simplest level, death is seen as punishment for Adam's original sin.

It is significant that in the very next verse, God says, "It is not good for man to be alone, I will make him a helpmate as his counterpart" (Genesis 2:18). On a simple level, this means that once the possibility of death exists, God must make arrangements for the continuation of the species. When the possibility of death came into existence, then Adam would have to have a wife if mankind was not to become extinct with his death.

However, this can also be understood on a much deeper level. From a number of Midrashic sources, we see that the spiritual realm is looked upon as masculine, while the physical world is feminine. Thus, in the overall scheme of creation, the spiritual realm fertilizes the physical while the physical realm acts as the womb, through which God's purpose is brought to fruition.

Life, of course, is the connection of the body and the soul. Since the body, as part of the physical realm, is feminine and the soul masculine, death is a separation of the masculine from the feminine. Hence, after the possibility of death came into existence in the world, God said, "It is not good for man to be alone"—it is not good for the soul, the masculine component of the body-soul unit, to be isolated from bodily existence through death.

Thus, there are two male-female relationships that a person can have. One is immortality, while the other is marriage. . . .

If life itself is a male-female relationship, then after man ate from the Tree of Knowledge and damaged this relationship, death was inevitable. It was for this reason that death was punishment for the first sin.

The World to Come, however, is seen as a time when all the effects of Adam's sin will be eradicated. Thus, the relationship between body and soul will also be perfected. Therefore, it will . . . be a time when man will live immortally with body and soul together.

ARYEH KAPLAN

❖

And *Abram went down to Egypt* (Genesis 12:10).
Rabbi Shim'on said:
"Come and see:
Everything has secret wisdom.
This verse hints at wisdom and the levels down below,
to the depths of which Abraham descended.
He knew them but did not become attached.
He returned to face his Lord,
was not seduced by them like Adam,
was not seduced by them like Noah.

"When Adam reached that level,
he was seduced by the serpent
and dragged Death into the world.

"When Noah descended to that level,
what is written?
'He drank of the wine and became drunk
and uncovered himself within his tent'
     (Genesis 9:21) . . .

"But what is written of Abraham?
'Abram went up from Egypt'
     (Genesis 13:1).
He went up and did not come down.
He returned to his domain,
the high rung he had grasped before."

ZOHAR (*trans. Daniel Chanan Matt*)

❖

WHEN AN individual realizes that death can occur at any moment without warning . . . and is unaware of when he himself will be called to give account, it is fitting that he rise up and hasten to prepare provisions for his journey. For no individual is assured of continued life for even a single day. . . .

Similarly, when a person realizes that after his death his eyes will cease to function, how remorseful will he then be with respect to his earlier habits. While he is still able to see he will say to himself: "Why have I not used my eyes for the purpose of studying Torah by abstaining from sleep?" Therefore, while the spirit of life is still within him, a person should flee from death and cleave to the Torah, the Tree of Life. . . .

When Adam sinned he became clothed in a thick material body which prevents the soul from envisioning the supernal holiness on high. By means of his death a person divests himself of this "clothing" and dons spiritual garments which are fashioned out of the deeds and precepts which he performed during the course of his lifetime. In this way, he is privileged to behold and to delight in the light of supernal life. Inasmuch as death effects the mending of a righteous individual's soul, by virtue of which he is privileged to be clothed in these spiritual garments, a wicked individual who fears death ought to turn in repentance.

ELIJAH DE VIDAS (trans. Lawrence Fine)

❖

We laid [Rabbi Nachman of Bratzlav] on the bed
dressed in his fine silk robe. He told Reb Shimon to arrange
his clothes and button his sleeves so that his shirt should
not protrude from the robe. He mentioned to Reb Shimon
to arrange it properly.

He then told us to wash the coughed-up blood from his
beard. We cleaned him, and he lay in bed feeling very free.

He took a small ball of wax and rolled it between his fingers, as he often did toward his last days when thinking deep
thoughts. Even in this last hour his thoughts were flying
through awesome worlds, and he rolled this ball of candlewax
between his fingers with great lucidity of mind. . . .

It was not long before he passed away and was gathered
to his fathers in great holiness and purity. Bright and clear,
he passed away without any confusion whatsoever, without
a single untoward gesture, in a state of awesome
calmness. . . .

But the true significance of his death cannot be compre-
hended at all. Whoever understands even a small amount
of his greatness from his works, conversations and tales . . .
will understand that it is utterly impossible to speak of such
a wondrously unique passing from this world.

NATHAN HERTZ OF NEMEROV (*trans. Aryeh Kaplan*)

❖

Rabbi Asher of Stolyn told:

My teacher, Rabbi Shelomo [of Karlin], used to say: "I

have to prepare what I shall have to do in hell," for he was certain that no better end was in store for him. Now, when his soul ascended after death, and the serving angels received him joyfully, to guide him to the highest paradise, he refused to go with them. "They are making fun of me," he said. "This cannot be the world of truth." At last the Divine Presence herself said to him: "Come my son! Out of mercy, I shall give you of my treasure." Then he gave in and was content.

MARTIN BUBER

❖

OUR SAGES teach us that the Torah was created two thousand years before the world.

This is difficult to understand, since the Torah contains the accounts of many events that happened after creation. How then can the Torah speak of creation, Adam and Eve, Noah, the holy Patriarchs, and all the other happenings recorded in the Torah? All these things had not yet happened [when the Torah was written].

This is even more difficult to understand when we realize that death only came into existence as a result of Adam's sin. If Adam had not sinned, death would not exist.

[Before Adam sinned, however], he had absolute free will. This being so, how can the concept of death appear in the Torah [written two thousand years before creation]? How can the Torah state that a particular individual died? How can we find such passages as, "When a man dies in a tent" (Numbers 19:14) . . . ?

Actually, when the Torah was first created, it was a mixture of letters. The letters of the Torah were not yet combined into words as they are now. . . .

Whenever anything then happened in the world, these letters were combined, and the words were recombined to form the account.

This was true of the account of creation, and the story of Adam and Eve. The letters combined with each other, forming the words that told this story. Similarly, when an individual died, a combination of letters was formed, saying that he had died. The same was true of the rest of the Torah.

THE BAAL SHEM TOV (*trans. Aryeh Kaplan*)

JOY

WHEN A man is continually in a state of joy then he can easily set aside an hour during the day to talk to God with a broken heart, and to pour out his soul before Him. But when a man is sad and depressed it is difficult for him to isolate himself with God, and to speak openly to Him. Therefore a man has to make an effort to be joyous always. . . .

Through depressions and sadness a man can forget who he really is. Therefore it is necessary to be continually in a state of joy, no matter what low level a person may be at. Through joy also, one can give renewed life to another. For there are people who suffer greatly and they walk around full of suffering and worry. When someone approaches them with a happy face he is able to give them renewed life. To do this is not some empty matter but an exceedingly great thing. . . .

Just as when people are happy and dance, they snatch up those who are standing at the side feeling in low spirits and depressed, and force them into the whirl of the dance, so it is with joy itself. For when a man rejoices then depression and suffering stand at the side. A person should try and chase after his depression and force it into the rejoicing, so that the depression itself is turned into joy.

NACHMAN OF BRATZLAV (*trans. Alan Unterman*)

❖

A PERSON ought to derive greater pleasure from the joy of serving God and fulfilling His commandments than from all the money in the world . . . no joy in the world may be compared with that of the commandments.

ELIJAH DE VIDAS (*trans. Lawrence Fine*)

❖

WHEN YOU want to pray to God for something, think of your soul as part of the Divine Presence, like a raindrop in the sea. Then pray for the needs of the Divine Presence.

You can have faith that your prayer will benefit the Divine Presence. Then, if you are properly attached to the Divine Presence, this influence will also be transmitted to you.

When a person is happy, he unconsciously claps his hands. This is because his joy spreads through his entire body. The same is true of the Divine Presence. Each influence is transmitted to each of its parts.

THE BAAL SHEM TOV (*trans. Aryeh Kaplan*)

❖

AFTER THE acceptance of the Blessing and after the delights bow and prostrate themselves before the awesome and sublime Throne of Glory, the Throne of Kingdom . . . whirls and revolves back from emanation to emanation to its origin [on the Cosmic Tree], resting between the two cherubs which are her arms.

This great outpouring—a joy to the inner souls and a delight to the spiritual bodies—was in effect when the land of Israel was inhabited and the holy nation dwelled in her. [The earthly] Temple is mirrored by [the celestial] Temple and [the] attendant High Priest is mirrored by a High Priest of holiness and purity, of fear and trembling, knowing how to direct perfect meditations to each of the outer and inner emanations, knowing how to draw forth the secret of the holy seraphim, awakening the Holy Spirit with the beauty of poetry and music. The singers [of the Temple], each according to their position and their perception, concentrate with their fingers upon the strings of the harp and the tones which awaken the song and the chant. They direct their hearts to the Omnipresent. The Blessing is stirred and the Divine Presence dwells upon them, each according to his worship and perception. . . . Happy is the eye that beholds all this.

ISAAC BEN JACOB HA-KOHEN (*trans. Ronald C. Kiener*)

❖

Joy COMES to a person when he experiences some great pleasure, or when he hears news or sees something that gives him pleasure. Joy is then derived from that thing. We therefore see that joy itself comes from the Universe of Pleasure, which is in itself undetectable.

This is very high, on a level that is called Holy. . . . It

then descends, step by step, until it comes to man in the Spirit of the Holy. . . .

THE MAGGID OF MEZERITCH (*trans. Aryeh Kaplan*)

❖

WE ARE taught, "The reward of a commandment is a commandment."

The Baal Shem Tov said that when a commandment is observed with joy, one has such great delight that this would be enough, even if there was no other reward. Actually, when you observe a commandment with joy, there is reward without limit.

ARYEH KAPLAN

❖

RABBI BUNAM [of Pzhysha] expounded: "In [Psalm 147:3] we read: 'who healeth the broken in heart . . .' Why are we told that? For it is a good thing to have a broken heart, and pleasing to God, as it is written: 'The sacrifices of God are a broken spirit . . .' [Psalm 51:19]. But further on in the psalm we read: 'and bindeth up their wounds.' God does not entirely heal those who have broken hearts. He only eases their suffering, lest it torment and deject them. For dejection is not good and not pleasing to God. A broken heart prepares man for the service of God, but dejection corrodes service. We must distinguish as carefully between the two, as between joy and wantonness; they are so easily confused, and yet are as far removed from one another as the ends of the earth."

MARTIN BUBER

❖

AND INASMUCH as all the heavenly spheres bring forth song out of their longing to cleave to God, so must a person also sing and praise God in order to gladden his Maker and to cleave to Him. For song facilitates cleaving to God in that a person recalls the many benevolent and compassionate things which He does for him. . . .

In connection with joy, there is a general rule that God enables the joyful to effect His unification—a privilege not accorded all people. The joy which a person brings to the fore during his prayer [particularly when he is in the synagogue or house of study] becomes a crown for the King of the Universe.

ELIJAH DE VIDAS (*trans. Lawrence Fine*)

❖

DEPRESSION IS the strongest Husk [evil] of all. We thus find that idolatry is called by a similar name. [The Hebrew word for sadness and depression is *atzav,* and the same word is used for idolatry] as we find, "Their idols (*atzav-eyhem* . . .) are silver and gold [the work of human hands]" (Psalms 115:4).

Depression thus has no relationship to God. Regarding God it is written, "Force and joy are in His place" (1 Chronicles 16:27). The Divine Presence therefore only rests on a place of joy.

MENACHEM MENDEL OF VITEBSK (*trans. Aryeh Kaplan*)

◇

WHEN HE was asked which was the right way, that of sorrow or that of joy, [Levi Yitzchak of Berditchov] said: "There are two kinds of sorrow and two kinds of joy. When a man broods over the misfortunes that have come upon him, when he cowers in a corner and despairs of help—that is a bad kind of sorrow, concerning which it is said: 'The Divine Presence does not dwell in a place of dejection.' The other kind is the honest grief of a man who knows what he lacks. The same is true of joy. He who is devoid of inner substance and, in the midst of his empty pleasures, does not feel it, nor tries to fill his lack, is a fool. But he who is truly joyful is like a man whose house has burned down, who feels his need deep in his soul and begins to build anew. Over every stone that is laid, his heart rejoices."

MARTIN BUBER

CHILDREN

Rabbi Isaac and Rabbi Judah were out on the road.
They reached the village of Sikhnin
and stayed there with a woman who had one little son
who went to school every day.
That day he left school and came home.
He saw these wise men.
His mother said to him, "Approach these distinguished
    men;
you will gain blessings from them!"
He approached them and suddenly turned back.
He said to his mother, "I don't want to go near them
because they haven't recited Shema today,
and I have been taught:
'Anyone who has not recited Shema at its proper time
is under a ban that entire day.'"

They heard this and were amazed.
Raising their hands, they blessed him.
They said, "Indeed, it is so!
Today we were engaged with a bride and groom
who did not have what they needed and were delaying their
    union.
There was no one to engage in helping them,

so we engaged, and we did not recite Shema at its proper
   time.
One who is busy doing a *mitzvah* [commandment] is
   exempt from another *mitzvah*."
Then they said, "My son, how did you know?"

He said, "I knew by the smell of your clothes when I came
   near you.". . .

Rabbi Judah said, "My son, what is the name of your
   father?"
The child was silent for a moment.
He rose and went over to his mother and kissed her.
He said, "Mother, these wise men have asked me about
   father.
Should I tell them?"
His mother said, "My son, have you tested them?"
He said, "I've tested them and found them lacking!"
His mother whispered to him, and he returned to them.
He said, "You have asked about father.
He has departed from the world,
but whenever holy devotees are walking on the road
he appears as a donkey driver behind them.
If you are so high and holy, how could you have missed him
following you as a donkey driver?
Ah, but right from the start I saw who you were,
and now I see through you!
For Father never sees a donkey and fails to goad it from
   behind
so he can share the yoke of Torah.

Since you weren't worthy enough for father to follow you,
I won't say who father is!". . .

They came and kissed him.
Rabbi Judah cried, and said:
"Rabbi Shim'on [bar Yochai], happy are you! Happy is the
     generation!
Because of you
even little schoolchildren are towering, invincible rocks!"

[The boy's] mother came and said to them,
"Masters, please look upon my son only with a good eye!"
They said to her, "Happy are you, worthy woman!
Singled out from among all women!
The Blessed Holy One has selected your portion,
raised your banner above all women of the world!". . .

[The boy] took the cup of blessing and began to bless. . . .
The cup stood firm and settled in his right hand
and he continued blessing.
At the end he said, "May it be the Will
that life be extended to one of these
from the Tree of Life, on which all life depends!
May the Blessed Holy One be surety for him!
May he find surety below to share his surety with the Holy
     King!"

Having finished blessing, he closed his eyes for a moment.
Then he opened them and said:

"Comrades, *shalom* to you from the good Lord who
   possesses all *shalom*!"
They were amazed and cried, and blessed him.

ZOHAR (*trans. Daniel Chanan Matt*)

❖

ON ROSH ha-Shanah in Uman shortly before his death,
[Rebbe Nachman of Bratzlav] was visited by his grandson
Yisrael, the son of his daughter Sarah. At the time, the
grandson was a very young child, around three or four years
old. The Rebbe was then suffering from the tuberculosis
that would take his life during the intermediate days . . . of
Sukkoth.

The Rebbe said to his grandson Yisrael, "Pray to God for
me so that I will become healthy again."

"Give me your pocket watch," replied the child, "and I
will pray for you."

"He's becoming a professional wonder worker already!"
exclaimed the Rebbe jokingly. With that, the Rebbe gave
the watch to the child.

The child then prayed, "God! God! Let grandpa get
better!"

The people standing there began to chuckle. The Rebbe
interrupted them and said, "This is how one must pray to
God. How can one pray differently?"

He was teaching that the way to pray is with absolute
simplicity, like a child before its parent, or like a person
speaking to a friend.

NACHMAN OF BRATZLAV (*trans. Aryeh Kaplan*)

❖

BEN AZAI said that those who do not have children are like unto those who shed blood and diminish the image of God in the world. Whereupon the rabbis said to him that some people preach well and practice well, others practice well but do not preach well, but Ben Azai the bachelor preaches well but does not practice what he preaches. "What can I do?" Ben Azai replied: "My soul is in love with the Torah. The world will have to be populated by others."

ALAN UNTERMAN

❖

[THE THIRD of] the three princes who are the three pillars to the [Heavenly] Throne . . . is Nashri'el, derived from the name of that [divine] emanation which is angry and chastises its children when they fail to conduct themselves along the straight path before their heavenly Father. But when they tip the scales toward merit by way of repentance, then they have peace and divine benevolence, and [the heavenly Mother] has mercy upon her children. . . . And then "the mother of the children is joyous, reclining on her beloved" [Psalms 113:9; Canticles 8:5].

ISAAC BEN JACOB HA-KOHEN (trans. Ronald C. Kiener)

❖

ONCE WHEN there was not a piece of bread in Rabbi Mendel [of Rymanov's] house, his son ran to him crying and complained his hunger was so great he could bear it no longer.

"Your hunger is not so great as all that," said his father. "For otherwise I should have something to quiet it."

The boy slunk off without a word. But before he reached the door, the rabbi saw a small coin lying on the table.

"I wronged you," he called out. "You are really very hungry indeed."

MARTIN BUBER

◇

WHENEVER RABBI David of Lelov came to a Jewish town he gathered all the children around him and gave each a little whistle. Then he packed them into the big wagon he used for traveling, and drove them all over town. The children whistled with might and main the entire time, and the entire time Rabbi David's face was wreathed in smiles.

MARTIN BUBER

◇

THE COMMANDMENTS . . . have a hidden part and a revealed part. The hidden part is our bringing pleasure to God through our observance of the commandments, since we have no way of detecting this. [The revealed part is] when we benefit ourselves, since this is visible.

This is the meaning of the verse, "Hidden things belong to the Lord our God, [but revealed things belong to us and to our children forever]" (Deuteronomy 34:22).

"Hidden things" allude to the hidden part of the commandment, and these "belong to the Lord our God." What we accomplish with relation to God is hidden from us.

"Revealed things belong to us and to our children," however, since the divine influence that we bring about is revealed to us.

LEVI YITZCHAK OF BERDITCHOV (*trans. Aryeh Kaplan*)

❖

WHEN RABBI Baer [the Maggid of Mezeritch] was five years old, a fire broke out in his father's house. Hearing his mother grieve and cry about this, he asked her: "Mother, do we have to be so unhappy because we have lost a house?"

"I am not grieving for the house," she said, "but for our family tree which burned up. It began with Rabbi Yohanan, the sandal-maker, the master in the Talmud."

"And what does that matter!" exclaimed the boy. "I shall get you a new family tree which begins with me!"

MARTIN BUBER

❖

EVERY ACT of unification constitutes an act of love; this is especially true given our current state of exile in which the divine union is severed and our Mother is in exile in this world. . . . For we must take it upon ourselves to restore the unity of God through our prayers and religious deeds. This may be compared to a son who loves his mother and who requests from his father food, raiment, and conjugal rights on behalf of his impoverished mother. He becomes exceedingly angry with his father and weeps on account of his mother's exile, reminding his father about the love which they once shared in their youth. . . . The children are responsible for awakening this love through their prayers.

ELIJAH DE VIDAS (*trans. Lawrence Fine*)

The Rabbi and His Only Son

THERE WAS a rabbi who was childless for some time until he was blessed with a son. He raised him lovingly, and when the young man was old enough, found him a proper bride. The son was given an upstairs room so he could continue his studies undisturbed, as was the custom of the well-to-do in that area. The son was conscientious. He spent his time in study and prayer. But he had the feeling that there was something missing in his life. Sometimes he didn't feel complete devotion when he prayed, or it seemed as if he missed the inner reason in his study. He spoke of this lack to two of his young comrades, and they suggested that he visit a certain Righteous Man, a *zaddik*. This young man had already reached the level where he'd become a small light in the world, by virtue of his good deeds.

The young man went and told his father about his feelings, that there was a certain tastelessness in his religious life, and that this lack bothered him. He didn't know what caused it, and wished to go and consult with this certain *zaddik* about whom he'd heard. His father did his best to discourage the son regarding this plan. He asked, "Why go to him? You yourself are a greater scholar than he is. And you come from a better family. It doesn't seem right for you to go to one such as he. Forget about it." The father continued in this manner till he succeeded in preventing the trip. And the son returned to his studies.

Some time later he was once again disturbed by this same problem, and again he consulted with his friends about the lack that he felt. As before, they suggested that he travel to see the *zaddik*. He told his father that he wished to go. His father tried to divert him, and persuaded and argued as before until he succeeded in preventing the trip. This occurred again and again, a number of times. Each time he would feel an internal emptiness that he longed to fill, yet he was not certain what was troubling him. Finally he went to his father and pleaded with him till his father could no longer refuse. Yet, because this was his only son, the rabbi did not want him to take the trip alone and decided to accompany him. To his son, he said, "All right, you may go, and I'll go with you. But you'll eventually see that he wasn't worth the trip."

They traveled by coach. Along the way, the father said: "If all goes well on this trip, we'll know it was meant to be. But if we start encountering troubles along the way, let us take that as a sign from Heaven that we weren't meant to go. In that case, we'll return home." Eventually they came to a bridge and the horse stumbled. The carriage was overturned, and they were nearly drowned. His father said, "You can see that this trip wasn't meant to be," and they turned around and went back. The son returned to his studies. But once again he felt this lack that he couldn't identify, and again he pleaded with his father until he obtained his father's consent, and they traveled together as before.

This time, as before, his father made it a condition that they would continue on this venture only as long as all went well, and that they would interpret difficulties along the way as a sign from Heaven that they were not to make this trip. As they were traveling, both the axles of the carriage broke. The rabbi said, "This is a sure sign that we weren't meant to take this trip. It is unnatural for both axles to break. Many times we have traveled in this coach, yet these things never happened." So they returned, and the young man went back to his holy ways. But the same problem revisited him. Again he became dejected by these feelings, and again he spoke to his friends of this matter. Their advice, as before, was that he really should go to see this *zaddik.* And he explained his great desire to his father, and his father gave in, and agreed to go. But this time the son said to his father, "Let's not interpret what happens along the way as signs from heaven. It is only natural that a horse will stumble now and then, or that an axle will break. Unless we encounter something really unusual that can't be ignored, let us complete this trip."

They traveled along the way, and when they got to an inn, they stopped for the night. There they met a businessman. They got into the sort of typical conversation that one has on the road, with casual encounters. They didn't mention where they were going because the rabbi was a little embarrassed by the whole affair, and by the fact that they were going such a distance just to visit a righteous man. They spoke of politics, and the affairs of the world. Without discussing things in depth, they moved from subject to subject till they found themselves talking about *zaddikim,* and where righteous people were to be found. The businessman mentioned a *zaddik* that he had heard of in a certain place, and then spoke of another one in another place, and still another one that people sometimes went to visit, or to ask for his blessing. And so they mentioned the name of the *zaddik* (that they were going to visit). To which, the businessman remarked, "Him? He's nothing! I just happen to be coming back from a visit with him myself, and I observed him in the act of a transgression!" The father then spoke to the young man, "You see, my son, what this man says in a passing manner, and he's coming from there." So they turned around and went home.

Soon thereafter, the son died. After he had died he appeared in a dream to the rabbi, his father. The rabbi saw him standing before him, very angry. He asked, "What is this anger?" The son replied that he should go to this same *zaddik* that the son had always wanted to visit, and he would explain to the father why the son was angry. The father woke up and dismissed what he had seen, as "just a dream." Then, some time later, he had the same dream again. He did not take it seriously, thinking that it was just because of his sadness at having lost his son. But when he had had this same dream three times, he was impressed. He set out to visit the *zaddik.* On his way he met the same businessman that he had met on the previous trip, when he had been traveling with his son. He recognized him, and said, "Didn't we once meet in an inn?"

The man said: "We certainly did!" And the rabbi was

surprised by the tone of his voice, and even more so by what the man said next, "If you want, I could swallow you!" "What are you saying?" asked the rabbi.

"Do you remember," said the man, "how you traveled with your son, and the first time the horse fell off the bridge and you returned? The next time the axles broke. And after that you met me. And I told you that the *zaddik* was nothing special? Well now that I've gotten rid of your son, you can go on with your visit. Your son was the Small Light in this world, and the *zaddik* is the Great Light, and if the two of them had gotten together, the Messiah would have come. But now that I've gotten rid of him, you can go on alone." And while he was speaking, he suddenly disappeared. The shocked rabbi found himself standing alone.

The rabbi then continued on his way to the *zaddik*. And he shouted, "Oh what a shame, oh what a shame for that which is lost and cannot be forgotten. May the blessed Lord bring back the dispersed very soon, Amen."

(The businessman was the Satan himself, that fooled them. Later, when he met the rabbi, he berated him for following his advice, for that is his custom.) May God save us from him.

NACHMAN OF BRATZLAV (*trans. Aryeh Kaplan*)

FAITH

$\mathbb{F}$AITH IS a very strong thing, and it can greatly fortify your life.

If you have faith, you have a source of comfort and inspiration, even when troubles strike. You realize that all troubles are ultimately for your good, and can be an atonement for your sins. You know that God will be good to you in the end, both in this world and in the next.

The faithless skeptic, on the other hand, has nowhere to turn when troubles strike. He is utterly alone, with neither comfort nor inspiration.

NACHMAN OF BRATZLAV (*trans. Aryeh Kaplan*)

❖

$\mathbb{I}$ HEARD that Rabbi Nachman once encouraged a person who was greatly confused about his beliefs.

Rabbi Nachman told him, "It is written that all creation was brought into being only because of people like you. God saw that there would be people who would cling to our holy faith, suffering greatly because of the confusion and doubts that constantly would plague them. He perceived that they would overcome these doubts and remain strong in their beliefs. It was because of this that God brought forth all creation."

This individual was greatly strengthened and was subsequently unperturbed when he had these confusing thoughts.

On numerous other occasions, Rabbi Nachman said that the creation was mainly for the sake of faith. It is thus written, "All his works are through faith" (Psalm 33:4).

NATHAN HERTZ OF NEMEROV (*trans. Aryeh Kaplan*)

❖

SINCE FAITH (*emunah*) stems from Eyn Sof [the Boundless One], one says *amen*, and in so doing he is like one who says "in Faith (*be-emunah*), the Trainer (*ha-omen*) increases the Confidence (*imun*) from the Artisan (*oman*), by means of *amen*."

This means: *amen* increases Truth (*emet*) out of Faith (*emunah*). According to Rabbi Hiyya, *amen* causes Truth to grow forth from its origin so that it expresses God's Unity and Kingdom. Thus, *amen* draws the power from Faith to increase the power of Truth, which nourishes everything. Furthermore, he who answers *amen* in faith increases the Source of Blessing. He not only is the one who increases the blessing from [the sphere of] Blessing, but from the Source itself.

RABBI AZRIEL (*trans. Ronald C. Kiener*)

❖

FAITH AND reliance are two matters wherein the latter requires its counterpart while the former does not depend on the latter. For faith precedes reliance and endures in the heart of the believer even though reliance is not present. To exist, faith does not need reliance; therefore faith is not an indication of reliance. But reliance points to faith, for it is impossible for reliance to exist before faith, nor can it endure without faith.

All who trust are called believers, but not every believer can be called reliant, for faith is like a tree and reliance like a fruit. Now the fruit is dependent on the tree or the plant which nurtures it. But the tree or plant is not dependent on the fruit, for there are some trees and many plants which do not bear fruit. Nevertheless, fruit cannot exist without some tree or plant.

This is similar to piety, [for piety] is indicative of wisdom and it is impossible to be pious unless one is already wise. Thus [the sages] said: "A boor does not fear sin, nor is an ignoramus pious." But wisdom does not depend on piety, for it is possible to be both brilliant and evil.

And so it is with faith and reliance: every trusting person is a believer, for a man cannot have trust except in whom he believes has the ability to fulfill his own requests.

JACOB BEN SHESHET OF GERONA (*trans. Ronald C. Kiener*)

❖

THE PROPHET Isaiah, may he rest in peace, taught: "And their fear of Me is a commandment of men learned by rote"

[Isaiah 29:13]. From this we learn that a person must investigate and determine with inner certainty who it is that he worships and who it is that he reveres, just as King David commanded his son Solomon: "Know thou the God of thy father, and serve Him with a whole heart and with a willing mind . . ." [1 Chronicles 28:9]. The reason for doing so is that a person who serves God as "a commandment of men learned by rote" will worship Him off and on. Such an individual lacks complete faith. Should a heathen come along, or another such as himself, and contradict his faith by the use of proofs and contrived arguments, it is possible that he may become convinced. However, a person who serves God with knowledge of the heart will resist being overwhelmed whatsoever.

ELIJAH DE VIDAS (*trans. Lawrence Fine*)

❖

THE WORDS from the daily liturgy, "Our God and the God of our fathers," represent two complementary aspects of faith. When we say, "our God," we are referring to our own understanding of God. Since this is something that we can only come to on our own, it is a human parallel to the [cosmic sphere of Dominion]. . . . The "God of our fathers," on the other hand, is the [cosmic sphere of Loving-kindness] aspect of faith because it involves submitting to the authority of tradition, or to what is given to us. Again, the message is that true faith must develop without any interference from without. In order to be able to stand up against all possible challenges, however, it must be grounded in something that goes beyond our personal experience.

ARYEH KAPLAN

❖

ALTHOUGH HEAVENLY powers wanted to give Elijah, the Gaon of Vilna, mystical and theosophical secrets through the medium of daemons, who were masters of secret knowledge and princes of the Torah, without the necessity of human effort, he refused them. He said that on numerous occasions heavenly mentors came to him volunteering to hand over to him the mystical secrets of the Torah without any effort on his part and he refused to take any notice of them. He said: "I do not want what I acquire of God's holy teaching (Torah) to come to me through any intermediary of whatever kind. Instead I am completely dependent on God and what he wants to reveal to me of his Torah, through my own labor which I am engaged in with all my might. He will give me wisdom, and an understanding heart. In that way I shall know that I have found favor in His eyes."

ALAN UNTERMAN

❖

THE RABBI [Menachem Mendel] of Kotzk made this comment on certain *zaddikim* of his time: "They claim that, during the Feast of Booths, they saw the Seven Shepherds in their booth as guests. I rely on my faith. Faith is clearer than sight."

MARTIN BUBER

◇

RABBI MOSHE Lieb [of Sasov] said: "There is no quality and there is no power of man that was created to no purpose. And even base and corrupt qualities can be uplifted to serve God. When, for example, haughty self-assurance is uplifted it changes into a high assurance in the ways of God. But to what end can the denial of God have been created? This too can be uplifted through deeds of charity. For if someone comes to you and asks your help, you shall not turn him off with pious words, saying: 'Have faith and take your troubles to God!' You shall act as if there were no God, as if there were only one person in all the world who could help this man—only yourself."

MARTIN BUBER

◇

RABBI MENDEL of Rymanov was asked how to interpret the words God added when he told Moses that the people were to gather a day's portion of manna every day: ". . . that I may prove them whether they will walk in my law or not."

He explained: "If you ask even a very simple man whether he believes that God is the only God in the world, he will give the emphatic answer: 'How can you ask! Do not all creatures know that He is the only one in the world!'

But should you ask him if he trusts that the Creator will see to it that he has all that he needs, he will be taken aback and after a while he will say: 'Well, I guess I haven't reached that rung yet.'

"But in reality belief and trust are linked, and one cannot exist without the other. He who firmly believes, trusts completely. But if anyone—God forbid—has not perfect confidence in God, his belief will be faint as well. That is why God says: 'I will cause to rain bread from heaven for you'; that means 'I *can* cause bread to rain from heaven for you.' But he who goes in the path of my teachings, and that means he who has belief in me, and that means, he who has trust in me, gathers a day's portion every day and does not worry about the morrow."

MARTIN BUBER

CREATION

" 'LET THERE be light!' And there was light."
Every subject of the phrase "And there was" exists in this
   world and in the world that is coming.

Rabbi Isaac said,
"The light created by the Blessed Holy One in the act of
   creation
flared from one end of the world to the other
and was hidden away.
Why was it hidden away?
So the wicked of the world could not enjoy it
and the worlds would not enjoy it because of them.
It is stored away for the righteous,
for the righteous one!
As it is written:
'Light is sown for the righteous one,
joy for the upright in heart' (Psalms 97:11).
Then the worlds will be fragrant, and all will be one.
But until the day when the world that is coming arrives,
it is stored and hidden away. . . ."

Rabbi Judah said:
"If it were completely hidden

the world would not exist for even a moment!
Rather, it is hidden and sown like a seed
that gives birth to seeds and fruit.
Thereby the world is sustained.
Every single day, a ray of that light shines into the world
and keeps everything alive,
for with that ray the Blessed Holy One feeds the world.
And everywhere that Torah is studied at night
one thread-thin ray appears from that hidden light
and flows down upon those absorbed in her, as it is written:
'By day YHVH will enjoin His love;
in the night His song is with me' (Psalms 42:9),
as we have already established. . . .

"Since the first day, it has never been fully revealed,
but it plays a vital role in the world,
renewing every day the act of creation!"

ZOHAR (*trans. Daniel Chanan Matt*)

❖

A HUMAN craftsman can make an article, as, for example, when a silversmith takes broken pieces of silver and makes them into a utensil. When he does this, he certainly places his wisdom and effort into that article. Therefore, since the article is made by this craftsman, the power of the doer is in the deed.

After the deed is completed, and the article is completed, no more thought or effort need be put into it. The utensil remains as it is, without any attention on the part of the craftsman.

This is because the craftsman made "something out of something"—a useful article out of a piece of silver. Therefore, after it is completed, it no longer needs the craftsman, since it had existence even before it came to his hand.

This is not true, however, of God's handiwork. He created the universe "something out of nothing," since before creation all that existed was absolute nothingness. Therefore, even after creation, if God were to remove His attention for even an instant, all worlds would revert to the state of utter nothingness that existed before creation.

The main power that all things have to exist and endure comes from the original power that God placed in them when He created the universe. This consists of the letters of the Torah with which He created the world, as our sages teach us.

Thus, for example, [in the original act of creation] God said, "Let there be a firmament in the midst of the waters" (Genesis 1:6). Through the letters of this statement, the firmament came into existence. And even now, the heavens and the heavens of heaven endure and exist only as a result of these letters. If the sustenance of the Life Force contained in those letters were to be removed even for an instant, [the heavens] would revert to their original state of absolute nothingness, and would be as if they never existed. The same is true of all worlds, both on high and in the physical universe.

CHAIM OF OHALOV (*trans. Aryeh Kaplan*)

◈

GOD'S PURPOSE in creation was to bestow of His good to another.

God alone is true perfection, free of all deficiency, and there is no perfection comparable to Him. Any imaginable perfection, with the exception of God's, is therefore not true perfection. . . .

Since God desired to bestow good, a partial good would not be sufficient. The good that He bestows would have to be the ultimate good that His handiwork could accept. God alone, however, is the only true good, and therefore His beneficent desire would not be satisfied unless it could bestow that very good, namely the true perfect good that exists in His intrinsic essence. . . .

Therefore, even though created things cannot emulate God's perfection in their own right, the fact that they can be attached to Him allows them to partake of it, since they can be considered part of God's perfection as a result of their association with Him. They can thus derive pleasure from that true good to the greatest degree possible for them.

The purpose of all that was created was therefore to bring into existence a creature who could derive pleasure from God's own good, in a way that would be possible for it. . . .

When this creature earns perfection, it is fit to become drawn close to its Creator by virtue of resembling Him. Besides this, however, through its very earning of perfection it becomes drawn to Him continually—until, ultimately, its earning of perfection and its bonding in closeness to Him are all one condition.

MOSHE CHAIM LUZZATTO (*trans. Aryeh Kaplan*)

◇

GOD HAD absolutely no need to create the world. God Himself is absolute perfection, and He has no need for anything, even creation. Thus, to the best of our understanding, we can say that God created the universe for the purpose of bestowing good upon man.

God Himself calls His creation an act of goodness. It is for this reason that, at the end of the first six days of creation, after making man, the Torah says, "And God saw all that He had made and behold it was very good" (Genesis 1:35). We are being told that the creation of the universe was an expression of His goodness.

This is why God made man last in order of creation. All the world had to be prepared for man. God therefore tells us through His prophet, "I have made the earth, and have created man upon it" (Isaiah 45:12). For it is man who will ultimately be the recipient of God's goodness, thereby fulfilling God's purpose in creation.

The Talmud provides us with a parable about this: a king once built a beautiful palace, decorating it lavishly and stocking it with the best food and drink. When it was all finished, he invited his guests, saying, "If there are no guests, then what pleasure does the king have with all the good things that he has prepared?" After everything had been prepared, the guest—man—was brought into the world.

ARYEH KAPLAN

❖

RABBI ZUSYA said: "I would like to be able not to eat, but what can I do, since my Creator simply forces me to by the fact that he has created a mouth for me? Now surely God did not create anything in his world except to serve him alone, therefore why did he need to create a mouth to eat and such like, except that one can serve him with one's mouth? In everything in this world there is a spiritual essence which needs to be raised to God."

ALAN UNTERMAN

❖

[THERE ARE] seventy-three Names that were inscribed in God's arm before the world was created. Upon finding Himself alone, He yearned to create the universe. . . .

[Thus] God extracted one of the seventy-three Names and from it He drew forth three droplets of water and the entire world filled with water, which He then placed below Himself. For it is written, "And the wind of God hovered above the surface of the water" (Genesis 1:2).

He extracted a second Name and drew forth from it three droplets of light and the entire world became permeated with light. This is the sevenfold light, as Scripture states: "Let there be light" (Genesis 1:3). He set the light to

His left, for the verse states HE COVERS HIMSELF WITH
LIGHT, and one always covers oneself from the left side.

He extracted a third Name and from it drew forth three
droplets of fire. The entire world filled with fire, which He
then placed to His right. For it is written, "From His right
side is a burning law for them" (Deuteronomy 33:2).

Light, fire, and water—all were created from the Wisdom of Torah.

RABBI AZRIEL (*trans. Ronald C. Kiener*)

❖

GOD is not like a human worker. A human worker can
acquire knowledge now that he did not have before. This
knowledge is something new for him that he acquires.

A human worker, furthermore, has needs. He may, for
example, need a place in which to live. When he attains
enough knowledge to build a house, he does so.

God's knowledge, however, is part of His Essence, and is
not acquired. God, furthermore, does not have any needs.

Therefore, when God desired to create the world, this
desire did not suddenly come into existence. Just as God
Himself always existed, so did this Will [and desire]. From
the very beginning, He had a desire to create the world
precisely at the time that it was brought into being, and not
before.

When God created the world, He did so at exactly the
right time and season. His original intention was to create
it precisely at that time, and only at that time. Creation
therefore did not involve any change of God's mind.

THE BAAL SHEM TOV (*trans. Aryeh Kaplan*)

◈

RABBI [SIMHA Bunam of Pzhysha] taught: "This is how we must interpret the first words in the Scriptures: 'In the beginning of God's creation of the heaven and the earth.' For even now, the world is still in a state of creation. When a craftsman makes a tool and it is finished, it does not require him any longer. Not so with the world! Day after day, instant after instant, the world requires the renewal of the powers of the primordial word through which it was created, and if the power of these powers were withdrawn from it for a single moment, it would lapse into [chaos]."

MARTIN BUBER

◈

RABBI SCHNEUR Zalman taught: "Everyone who has insight into the matter will understand clearly that everything created and having being is as absolute naught with regard to the Activating Force, which is in all created being. This force constitutes its reality and draws it forth from absolute nothingness to being. The fact that all created things seem to have existence and being in their own right is because we can neither conceive nor see, with our physical eyes, the Force of God which is in the created world. Were the eye able to see and conceive the vitality and spirituality in each created thing, which flows through it from its divine source, then the physicality, materiality, and substantiality of the created world would not be seen at all; because apart from the spiritual dimension it is absolute nothingness. There is really nothing in existence besides God."

ALAN UNTERMAN

◈

THEY ASKED Rabbi Barukh [of Mezbizh]: "In the hymn, God is called 'Creator of remedies, awful in praises, lord of wonders.' Why? Why should remedies stand next to wonders and even precede them?" He answered: "God does not want to be praised as the lord of supernatural miracles. And so here, through the mention of remedies, nature is introduced and put first. But the truth is that everything is a miracle and wonder."

MARTIN BUBER

GLOSSARY

COSMIC TREE   The central emblem of the "worlds" or stages of meditation on the "ascent" to the Divine. (See illustration on page 43.)

EL SHADDAI   One of the names of God, alluding to His omnipotence.

EVIL URGE   The dark side of human nature, often metaphorically portrayed as the tempter.

EYN SOF (lit. "without end")   One of the names of God, alluding to His boundlessness and voidness.

GAON   A sage.

HASID (plural, Hasidim)   A follower of the path of prayer and ecstasy known as Hasidism.

HASIDISM   A sect founded in eighteenth-century eastern Europe by Israel Baal Shem Tov, also known as the Besht (a Hebrew acronym for "Master of the Holy Name").

KABBALAH   The mystical teachings of Judaism.

KAVANAH (plural, kavanoth)   Concentrated absorption in meditation; sometimes used to describe the form of prayer used to achieve absorption.

MAGGID (plural, maggidim)   Preacher; spirit guide.

MIKVAH   Ritual immersion or bath, performed by both women and men.

MITZVAH (plural, mitzvoth)   Commandment.

PERMUTATION OF LETTERS   A meditation technique interchanging Hebrew letters of a word or phrase for recitation combined with specific breathing exercises.

REBBE   "Old teacher"; a diminutive form of *rabbi*.

SEPHIROTH (singular, sephirah)   The ten stages of meditation on the Cosmic Tree, embodied in color and geometric forms used for vizualization. (See illustration on page 43.)

SHEKHINAH   The female aspect of God.

SHEMA   A daily prayer used in meditation, beginning, "Hear O Israel, the Lord is our God, the Lord is One."

TALLIT   Prayer shawl.

TALMUD   Redaction of the Jewish Oral Law, second only to the Bible in importance.

TEFILLIN   Phylacteries; small square leather boxes containing parchments with scriptural passages, worn on the left arm and the head during prayer.

TETRAGRAMMATON   YHVH, the four Hebrew letters of the secret name of God, permuted in meditation. (See illustration on page 56.)

TORAH   The first five books of the Hebrew Bible; Pentateuch. Generally, the body of Jewish wisdom and law.

UNIFICATION   Hebrew letter permutations of the various names of God; *yichud*.

YHVH   Tetragrammaton; the secret four-letter name of God.

YICHUD (plural, yichudim)   "Unification," a meditation technique permuting Hebrew letters.

ZADDIK (plural, zaddikim)   Holy man.

Sources

The Aryeh Kaplan Reader, by Aryeh Kaplan (Brooklyn: Mesorah Publications, 1990). Excerpts reprinted by permission.

The Bahir, by Aryeh Kaplan (York Beach, Me.: Samuel Weiser, 1989). Excerpts reprinted by permission of Samuel Weiser, Inc., York Beach, ME 03910.

The Early Kabbalah, edited by Joseph Dan and translated by Ronald C. Kiener (Mahwah, N.J.: Paulist Press, 1986). Excerpts reprinted by permission of Paulist Press.

Gems of Rabbi Nachman, by Aryeh Kaplan (Jerusalem: Breslover Yeshiva Press, 1980).

Inner Space, by Aryeh Kaplan (Brooklyn: Maznaim Publishing Corp., 1990). © Maznaim Publishing Corp., Brooklyn, N.Y. Excerpts reprinted by permission.

Kabbalah: The Way of the Jewish Mystic, by Perle Epstein (Boston: Shambhala Publications, 1988).

The Light Beyond: Adventures in Hassidic Thought, by Aryeh Kaplan (Brooklyn: Maznaim Publishing Corp., 1981). © Maznaim Publishing Corp., Brooklyn, N.Y. Excerpts reprinted by permission.

Meditation and Kabbalah, by Aryeh Kaplan (York Beach, Me.: Samuel Weiser, 1986). Excerpts reprinted by permission of Samuel Weiser, Inc., York Beach, ME 03910.

"Psychological Aspects of Early Hasidic Literature," by Siegmund Hurwitz, in *Timeless Documents of the Soul,* edited by Helmuth Jacobsohn (Evanston, Ill.: Northwestern University Press, 1968), p. 194.

Safed Spirituality: Rules of Mystical Piety, The Beginning of Wisdom, translated by Lawrence Fine (Mahwah, N.J.: Paulist Press, 1984). © 1984 by Lawrence Fine. Excerpts reprinted by permission of Paulist Press.

Tales of the Hasidim: The Early Masters, by Martin Buber (New York: Pantheon Books, 1975). Copyright 1947, 1948 and renewed 1975 by Schocken Books, Inc. Excerpts reprinted by permission of Schocken Books, published by Pantheon Books, a division of Random House, Inc.

Tales of the Hasidim: The Later Masters, by Martin Buber (New York: Pantheon Books, 1975). Copyright 1947, 1948 and renewed 1975 by Schocken Books, Inc. Excerpts reprinted by permission of Schocken Books, published by Pantheon Books, a division of Random House, Inc.

The Way of God, by Moshe Chaim Luzzatto, translated by Aryeh Kaplan (New York: Philip Feldheim Publishers, 1983), pp. 37, 39.

The Wisdom of the Jewish Mystics, by Alan Unterman (London: Sheldon Press, 1976). Excerpts reproduced by kind permission of SPCK, London.

The World of Hasidism, by Harry M. Rabinowicz (Hartford, Conn.: Hartmore House, 1970), pp. 53–54 .

Zohar: The Book of Enlightenment, translated by Daniel Chanan Matt (Mahwah, N.J.: Paulist Press, 1983). © 1983 by Daniel Chanan Matt. Excerpts reprinted by permission of Paulist Press.